The Yorkshire Dales

A Landscape Through Time

Robert White

GREAT NORTHERN

To Hilary, Emily and Nikki

Published in 2005 in a new edition by
Great Northern Books
PO Box 213, Ilkley, LS29 9WS

First published in 1997 as the Yorkshire Dales volume in the
English Heritage/Batsford "Landscapes through Time" series.

© Robert White 1997, 2005

ISBN: 1 905080 05 0

Printed by The Amadeus Press Limited, Bradford, West Yorkshire.

Contents

Illustrations

Colour plates

Acknowledgments

This first edition of this book was published by Batsford in a series sponsored by English Heritage. I am grateful to David Joy, Colin Speakman of the Yorkshire Dales Society, and the Yorkshire Dales National Park Authority for their support for a third edition and for enabling me to update the text to include some of the results of surveys and research undertaken or published since 2002. Like the previous editions, this book would not have been possible without the work of the numerous archaeologists who have studied and written about the archaeological sites and historic landscapes of the Yorkshire Dales. I am particularly grateful to Pete Horne and Dave Macleod of English Heritage for their work on the Yorkshire Dales Mapping Project, organised by the then Royal Commission on the Historical Monuments of England, which provided a systematic, desk-based analysis of aerial photographs of the area. This survey, together with an analysis of the first edition Ordnance Survey 1:10,560 maps also carried out as part of the Yorkshire Dales Project, the published and unpublished results of fieldwork by numerous individuals and organisations, paid and unpaid, and collections of aerial and ground photographs and historic maps, now forms the basis of the Historic Environment Record (HER) maintained by the National Park Authority. The HER is an important source of information in its own right for all those studying the historic environment of the National Park as well as an essential resource for the protection and management of the landscape and I am grateful to all those who have contributed to it.

The following individuals and institutions have kindly given permission to reproduce drawings and photographs: Tom Lord 8 and colour plate 1; John Gilks 12; Ed Dennison 40; Mike Gill and the Northern Mine Research Society 59; Lawrence Barker 62; Sallie Bassham 64; the Earby Mine Museum 67; and the North Yorkshire County Record Office colour plate 13. Figures 21, 33, 34, 42, 52, 55 and 57 are based on illustrations by Graham Webster, the Yorkshire Museum, Percival Turnbull, Stephen Moorhouse, Vera Chapman, Graham Darlington and Mike Gill. Colour plate 9 is by Judith Dobie of English Heritage. The aerial photographs were taken by the author with the exception of 20 which is by Paul Chadwick; and 22 and 43 which are reproduced by permission of the Cambridge University Committee for Aerial Photography. Other illustrations are from the collections of the author and the National Park Authority, including 76 by Chris Partrick, 78 by Roger Simpson of Northern Archaeological Associates, 84 by Jonathan Ratter, 86 by Stephen Haigh and colour plate 16 by Les Turner of EDAS.

I am grateful to Chris Lyall-Grant, Graeme Barker, Lawrence Barker, Ed Dennison, Jonathan Ratter and David Wade for their comments on drafts of the first edition.

INTRODUCTION

Austere, beautiful, oppressive, romantic: no two people have quite the same impression of the Yorkshire Dales. To some it is a wild landscape of bleak peat bog covered moors dominated by wind and driving rain; to others a geological and botanical paradise of weathered limestone pavement where green shade-loving plants peep through a maze of open clefts or grykes. The narrow gills and wide valleys with rushing streams and slower flowing rivers crossed by high arched stone bridges; the thousands of kilometres of dry-stone walls, some climbing nearly vertical slopes in arrow straight lines or bounding narrow grass surfaced lanes; the hundreds of small field barns which punctuate herb-rich hay meadows; the long, low, stone roofed farmhouses with small, mullioned windows and dated lintels; the scars of ancient lead mines and modern limestone quarries; the dry, springy turf of limestone pastures grazed by black-headed ewes and their lambs; and red grouse in purple heather moorlands; all these combine to create the character of the Yorkshire Dales landscape.

All have one thing in common: they are the result of a partnership between mankind and nature. Over millions of years nature created the basic landforms of fells, dales and rivers: the pattern of meadows and moorland, farms and villages, walls and woodland that covers these landforms, creating the landscape we see today, owes much to the work of people over little more than 12,000 years. No evidence of earlier human activity has been found in the Dales: any traces which may have existed are likely to have been destroyed during the last glaciation. The peat bogs on the high moors are a product of human clearance of the natural forest cover; the intricate network of dry-stone walls is a result of stone clearance and land division for arable and pastoral farming; the hay meadows and field barns represent a highly specialised response to the problem of overwintering cattle in a harsh upland climate; the prevalence of red grouse and heather moorland an increasingly commercial response to the demands of a leisure pursuit.

Traditionally archaeologists and historians have divided these 12,000 years into periods. The earlier or prehistoric periods - the Palaeolithic, Mesolithic, Neolithic, Bronze and Iron Ages - are based largely on apparent technological advances; the historic periods - Roman, Dark Ages, medieval and post-medieval - reflect documented administrative as well as social changes (1). The slower rate of change in the past means that the boundaries between the different periods are often indistinct. Even today, after a period of unprecedented development, the majority of the Dales population lives in houses built before the invention of the car. The Yorkshire Dales landscape does not convey an impression of rapid change - there are no hallmarks of the late twentieth century such as motorways, large industrial complexes or housing estates. But change is occurring. Quarrying is no longer a small-scale labour intensive industry; modern, synthetic materials are altering the appearance of farms and villages; tourism is now the major industry. Even the social structure is changing as the young move out of the area to find homes and jobs and retired 'offcomers' move in.

Similar changes have occurred in the past, some slowly, others more dramatically. Many Dales families emigrated to Lancashire and further afield as the lead industry declined. Textile manufacturing has come and gone, while the original effect of the sheer size of the defences of the Roman fort at Bainbridge or the now ruined remains of Richmond Castle and Bolton Abbey, still impressive today, must have been awe-inspiring to peasants living in small thatched wooden hovels.

Each generation has utilised, destroyed or sometimes just avoided the works of their predecessors so within the landscape of the Yorkshire Dales we can see traces of the successes and failures of 12,000 years of human activity. Some traces are obvious, others less so. The main aim of this book is to draw attention to mankind's role in the creation of the present-day Dales landscape but as the appearance of the countryside is conditioned by the underlying rocks, it begins with an outline of the area's geology and topography.

To enable the reader to locate places named in the text, Ordnance Survey grid references are given in the index.

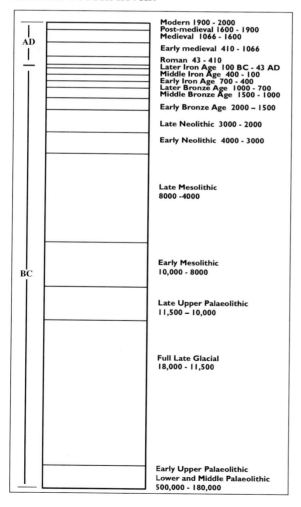

Modern 1900 - 2000
Post-medieval 1600 - 1900
Medieval 1066 - 1600
Early medieval 410 - 1066
Roman 43 - 410
Later Iron Age 100 BC - 43 AD
Middle Iron Age 400 - 100
Early Iron Age 700 - 400
Later Bronze Age 1000 - 700
Middle Bronze Age 1500 - 1000
Early Bronze Age 2000 – 1500
Late Neolithic 3000 - 2000
Early Neolithic 4000 - 3000
Late Mesolithic 8000 -4000
Early Mesolithic 10,000 - 8000
Late Upper Palaeolithic 11,500 – 10,000
Full Late Glacial 18,000 - 11,500
Early Upper Palaeolithic
Lower and Middle Palaeolithic 500,000 - 180,000

AD

BC

1. A time line showing archaeological periods and their approximate duration.

1
TROPICAL SEAS AND ICE SHEETS

A glance at a map of the Yorkshire Dales shows that the area is aptly named. The peaks rise to over 700m (2300ft) above sea level and large areas are over 600m (2000ft) but the eye is attracted to the 'dales', a Norse word for valley, which dissect the 'moors' or 'fells'.

The rocks which dominate this landscape were laid down as marine sediments during Carboniferous times. This geological period began about 350 million years ago and lasted for some 80 million years. Older rocks survive in the Howgill Fells where erosion has produced a distinct and dramatic landscape of smooth, rounded hills with long shoulders, dissected by deep, steep-sided valleys. Rocks similar to those found in the Howgill Fells underlie the Carboniferous rocks and are visible at the surface in small though economically important inliers in mid-Ribblesdale (**2**).

Changes in sea level were mainly responsible for the different types of rock formed during the Carboniferous period. The Great Scar Limestone, the youngest of these rocks, was formed by the slow deposition of shell debris and chemical precipitates upon the floor of a shallow tropical sea. Minor breaks in this accumulation are indicated by bedding planes and some thin bands of shale. Over millions of years the sediments were compressed and then recrystallised or metamorphosed into a very strong rock which is resistant to most forms of erosion. Like other limestones this is scarcely affected by pure water, but when rainwater

absorbs carbon dioxide it becomes slightly acidic and then the rock is slowly dissolved and removed in solution. Carbon dioxide is given off by plants and animals: the richer the surface vegetation the greater the amount of available gas and thus the greater the acidity of both rainwater and surface water and the faster the limestone is dissolved.

The principal outcrops of Great Scar Limestone and its distinctive landforms, technically known as 'karst', lie in the south-west part of the Dales, between Kingsdale and Wharfedale, an area historically known as Craven. Here it forms a wide, sweeping, now largely treeless landscape with thin calcareous soils and short green-turfed pastures subdivided by white dry-stone walls, and with dramatic outcrops of bare rock, either as steep cliffs known as 'scars' or as seemingly barren, but lichen-covered, limestone pavements (**3**). The distinctive profiles of the Three Peaks of Ingleborough, Whernside and Pen-y-Ghent rise above this karst landscape. Streams flowing off the hills disappear through sinkholes into a complex network of underground passages, some to reappear as springs. The limestone has been quarried for centuries. Its purity means that it is very important for the chemical industry but today the main product is aggregate for the construction industry.

Limestone is also a main constituent of the Yoredale Series rocks which overlie the Great Scar Limestone. Deltas emerging from rivers

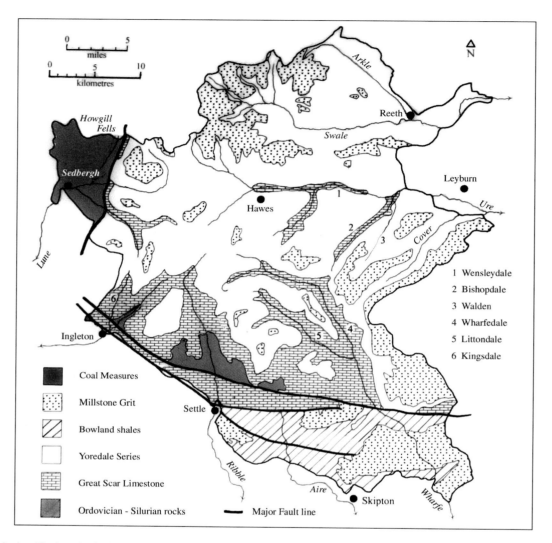

2 A simplified geological map of the Yorkshire Dales National Park, showing the principal rock outcrops and the main fault lines.

eroding the landmass to the north dropped muds and sands into the seas in which these rocks were formed. Periodic earth movements influenced both sea depth and delta activity, resulting in the rhythmic succession of deposits of limestone, shale and sandstone, the latter sometimes overlain by a thin coal seam, followed by limestone, shale and sandstone .... which together form the Yoredale Series.

These are nearly horizontally bedded, dipping only slightly north-east. Erosion has created distinctive step-like terraces along the valley sides. This is clearly seen in Wensleydale and Pen-y-Ghent Gill where the hard limestone scars stand out like the risers of a giant staircase with the easily weathered shales the treads (**4**). The scars, and the steep scree slopes immediately beneath them, are sometimes clothed with long narrow woods of oak and ash. Numerous small streams cascade down these terraces, the lips of the limestone outcrops creating the waterfalls which are such a feature of the northern dales. Some, like Hardraw Force and Whitfield Gill Force, are well known, others not even named. Other waterfalls and rapids, such as Wainwath Force and Kisdon gorge in Swaledale, formed

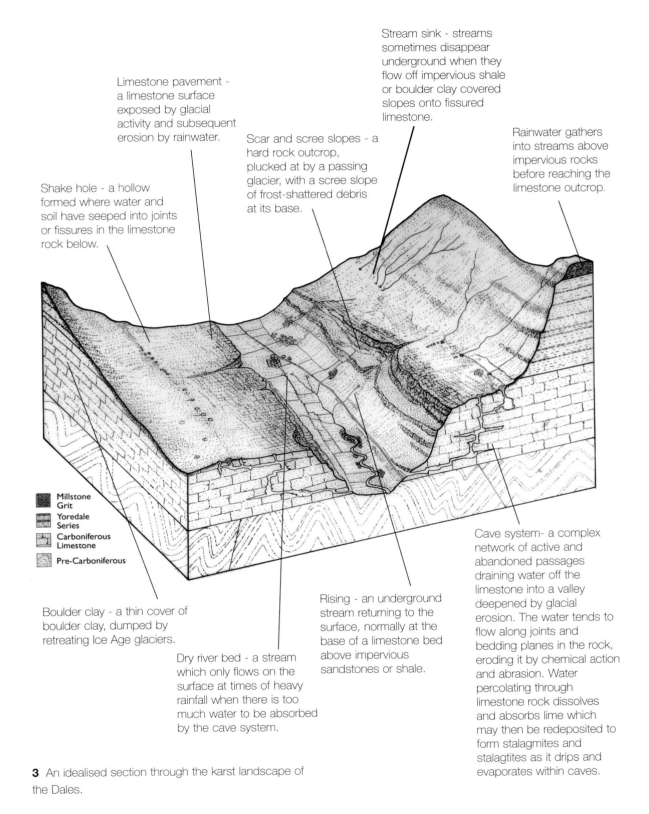

Limestone pavement - a limestone surface exposed by glacial activity and subsequent erosion by rainwater.

Stream sink - streams sometimes disappear underground when they flow off impervious shale or boulder clay covered slopes onto fissured limestone.

Scar and scree slopes - a hard rock outcrop, plucked at by a passing glacier, with a scree slope of frost-shattered debris at its base.

Rainwater gathers into streams above impervious rocks before reaching the limestone outcrop.

Shake hole - a hollow formed where water and soil have seeped into joints or fissures in the limestone rock below.

Millstone Grit

Yoredale Series

Carboniferous Limestone

Pre-Carboniferous

Boulder clay - a thin cover of boulder clay, dumped by retreating Ice Age glaciers.

Dry river bed - a stream which only flows on the surface at times of heavy rainfall when there is too much water to be absorbed by the cave system.

Rising - an underground stream returning to the surface, normally at the base of a limestone bed above impervious sandstones or shale.

Cave system- a complex network of active and abandoned passages draining water off the limestone into a valley deepened by glacial erosion. The water tends to flow along joints and bedding planes in the rock, eroding it by chemical action and abrasion. Water percolating through limestone rock dissolves and absorbs lime which may then be redeposited to form stalagmites and stalagtites as it drips and evaporates within caves.

3 An idealised section through the karst landscape of the Dales.

4 The step-like terraces at Dawson Close in Pen-y-Ghent Gill, formed by erosion of the Yoredale Series rocks, are utilised by an Iron Age settlement, a post-medieval sheepfold and rectangular structures of unknown date.

where the rivers themselves cut across the different rocks. The sandstone outcrops were quarried and mined to produce roofing slates and building stone. The coal seams were a valuable fuel supply, especially for the numerous small lime kilns built along the limestone outcrops for making lime to sweeten the pastures and for building purposes (**5**).

Shales and sandstones (some of the coarser sandstones are called gritstones) of the Millstone Grit Series dominate Nidderdale and the watersheds in the northern part of the Dales. On the high ground they create a much harsher landscape than the limestone country; a landscape of acid grass or heather moors with extensive cotton grass peat bogs where drainage is impeded. The sandstones and gritstones were also quarried as building stone and, as the name suggests, some beds were used for millstones. The Series includes thin coal beds, the best-known being worked at Tan Hill at the head of Arkengarthdale.

The metalliferous minerals which were so important to the economy of the area were formed during the major mountain building period which marked the end of the

5 This mid-nineteenth-century lime kiln used limestone extracted from the small quarry in the limestone outcrop behind (In the foreground) heather grows on thin acidic soils which have developed on sandstone.

Carboniferous Period. Hot saline liquids forced their way up through numerous faults and fissures in the Carboniferous rocks forming veins as they cooled and crystallised. The mineral deposits vary considerably in extent which made lead mining (Chapter 7) a highly speculative venture (6).

The Carboniferous rocks were subsequently covered by younger rocks and uplifted into a mountain chain. This has since eroded to such an extent that younger rocks no longer exist in the Dales.

The effects of the Ice Age

Major ice sheets have advanced and retreated across Britain at least three times in the last half million years bringing with them distinct forms of erosion and deposition. The effects of the latest, or Devensian, glaciation which began some 80,000 years ago, are the most apparent in the Yorkshire Dales. This glaciation was not constant - the generally bitter cold being occasionally broken by milder episodes called interstadials. We are living in an interstadial now, known as the Flandrian warm stage.

All of the Yorkshire Dales, with the exception of some of the higher peaks, were covered with ice during the last glaciation. Existing river valleys provided easy routes for massive ice sheets which spread from the north and west. With each advance of this ice, glaciers scoured and deepened the principal valleys into a characteristic U-shaped form (7), straightening out previously formed kinks and spurs. This is best seen at Kilnsey Crag, close to where a glacier moving down Littondale met the Wharfedale ice flow. Some high ground deflected the flows of ice. Buckden Pike diverted ice from Langstrothdale southwards down Wharfedale and north along Bishopdale, protecting in its lee the narrow, still V-shaped, valley of Walden Beck. This increased ice flow over-deepened the valley of Bishopdale. Then, as the ice sheets slowly retreated, the valley floor silted up as a glacial lake partly dammed by ice and debris from another glacier which, fed by

snow which had accumulated on the high ground around Baugh and Great Shunner Fells, continued to flow down Wensleydale. Lower Bishopdale is still very prone to flooding.

The ice sheets which covered the Yorkshire Dales carried with them vast quantities of rocks, sand and clay. As the ice retreated this mixture was dropped to form the boulder clay or drift deposits which blanket the floors and sides of many of the dales. Sometimes this boulder clay was partly overridden by the ice and moulded into drumlins. These small smooth egg-shaped hillocks are best seen in Upper Ribblesdale where they are aligned north-west - south-east in the direction of the main ice flow.

Terminal moraines, the deposits dropped at the front of a glacier, mark stages in the retreat of the ice sheets. The moraines sometimes blocked river valleys, as at Grinton and Gunnerside in Swaledale, causing lakes to form behind them. Some tributary streams entering the moraine lakes created deltas which, as at Buckden and Kettlewell in Upper Wharfedale, now provide drier settlement sites in otherwise flat and marshy valley bottoms.

Karst

Ice action, though powerful, is only part of the erosion history of the Dales. Water has been equally important, both as a physical erosive force and through chemical action, notably on the limestones which are soluble in acidic water. This can be clearly seen where boulders, known as erratics, carried from nearby Crummackdale during the last glaciation and deposited on top of limestone, have since protected the underlying rock from attack by rainwater. Some boulders at Norber are now perched on limestone blocks as much as 30cm (1ft) above the surrounding surface.

The most distinctive surface features of the karst are the areas of limestone pavement. Any overburden of soil, debris or weaker rock was scoured away by glacial activity leaving a smooth rock surface. Rainwater has seeped into the joints and other fractures of the limestone,

6 The deep gulleys left by mining beside Slei Gill in Arkengarthdale. The Gill cuts across three main veins, Tanner Rake, Scatter Scar and North Rake, which have been extensively worked by hushing.

slowly enlarging them by dissolving the rock walls to form gaping fissures, known as grykes. The blocks of bedrock between the grykes are called clints. Little soil has developed on the clints as limestone is almost totally eroded by solution but small pockets exist in some of the grykes. These, protected from sun and wind and from grazing animals, support plant communities of great botanical interest which belie the barren impression given by distant views. In some areas overlying walls indicate that man's agricultural practices have also played a part in the creation of limestone pavement by continuing or accelerating the process of soil erosion.

Scattered throughout the karst landscape are numerous other depressions where water has seeped into fissures in the limestone. Shakeholes, most of which are only a few metres wide and deep, are the hollows created where the soil and soft rocks overlying the limestone have been washed down the fissures. Cracks and tears in the vegetation and soil cover on the sides of shakeholes show that they are still actively developing. Shakeholes are most numerous where the overlying drift is two to three metres thick along buried shale-limestone boundaries. They should not be confused with the circular depressions, generally surrounded by small spoil heaps, left by shallow shaft mining for coal and lead.

Water from surface streams sometimes disappears into sinkholes, also known as swallow holes. The best-known example is Gaping Gill, south of Ingleborough, where Fell Beck plunges down a deep, open shaft into a massive underground chamber. Fifteen kilometres (9 miles) of caves and passages linked to this cavern have been mapped by geologists and cavers.

The cave systems were initially formed by rain and ground water slowly percolating down joints and cracks and along bedding planes until it found an exit or resurgence. Once a drainage route was established, dissolved material was

7 Glaciers scoured the Wharfe valley into the characteristic U-shape. Meadows and pastures line the valley floor and the medieval village of Kettlewell lies on either side of Cam Gill.

8 The 1870s excavations at Victoria Cave greatly increased the size of the cave entrance. They cut through more than 4m (12ft) of geological deposits, both inside and outside the cave, dumping the waste on large spoil heaps below the cave.

carried away and a labyrinth of interlacing passages and caves slowly created. Underground, water continues to erode and seek the lowest level and so sometimes cave passages are abandoned. The shapes of these fossil caves provide evidence of the levels of ancient water tables and valley floors and are important clues to the development of the landscape.

Frozen ground, a lack of flowing water and absence of plant life to increase the acidity of water meant that cave development virtually ceased during the ice advances. As the ice retreated the blocking of cave passages by ice and other debris sometimes forced meltwater to gouge out new courses and abandon old cave drainage systems. This process was accentuated by the deepening of valleys which meant that many caves were left isolated on hill sides.

These caves sometimes contain evidence for the evolution of the landscape. The best-known

example is Victoria Cave near Settle, so-called because it was supposedly discovered on Queen Victoria's coronation day in 1838 when Michael Horner crawled through a narrow passage into the hillside after his dog. Horner found some Roman coins and metalwork inside the cave which he showed to his employer, Joseph Jackson. Other material was later recovered by Jackson, and in the 1870s there was a major campaign at the cave (**8**). The excavators dug through the Roman occupation layers, through an upper cave-earth which contained quantities of bear, lynx, fox, badger, horse and red deer bones, and through a layer of pale laminated clays. Below these the cave-earth contained bones and teeth of hippopotamus, spotted hyena, narrow-nosed rhinoceros and straight-tusked elephant which in turn overlay further, dark, laminated clays. The clays probably represent flood deposits from melting icesheets. Modern scientific dating techniques have shown that the animals in the lower bone layer had lived during a warm inter-glacial period more than 120,000 years ago.

2
PREHISTORIC LANDSCAPES: HUNTER-GATHERERS TO HILLFORTS

About 13,500 years ago the climate began to improve and the ice sheets retreated leaving behind bare rock outcrops and deposits of mixed sand, clay, pebbles and boulders. Water filled the depressions left by the melting ice and formed ponds and lakes in valleys dammed by moraines. Gradually many of these filled in, first with silts and sands, then, as the water shallowed, with reeds and peat.

Waterlogged soil and peat deposits often contain well-preserved pollen grains. By extracting, identifying and counting pollen from various depths a picture can be formed of how vegetation and climate have developed over time. The bare ground was first colonised by mosses, lichens, grasses and herbs, forming an open, tundra environment, similar to parts of Iceland today. This was gradually invaded by shrubs, particularly dwarf varieties of willow, birch and juniper. As the climate continued to warm, these were succeeded by woodland, especially in the lower lying, better-drained and more sheltered valleys. This woodland varied

through the Dales, being influenced by soil, drainage and altitude. It was initially dominated by alder, pine and birch, with willow in the damper areas, and merged into open grassland on higher ground (**colour plate 1**). Here herds of animals such as reindeer, giant Irish elk and horse grazed, especially in summer, attracting predators such as wolf, arctic fox and bear.

The hunter-gatherers

Nomadic groups of humans were among the predators, though these early hunters have left little evidence of their presence. No remains of open-air camps have been found but the caves and overhangs of the limestone scars could have provided ready-made shelter. Surviving items from their 'tool kit' consist mainly of large, relatively simple, flint knives, axes and scrapers and carved antler harpoons, although wood and plant fibres and other animal products such as bones, hides and hair were no doubt also used. An antler harpoon point, found near the back of Victoria Cave, has recently been dated to about 11,000 years ago (**9**). This is proof that people were present in the area but not that they were occupying the cave: the harpoon may have been lost while hunting. A wounded quarry, perhaps a deer, could have eluded capture and subsequently sought shelter in the cave or been dragged into it by scavengers such as hyenas.

As the amount of woodland increased, red deer, roe deer, wild boar and giant ox (aurochs) added to the potential human food supply.

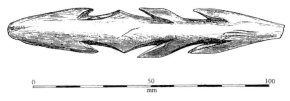

0   50   100
           mm

9 An antler harpoon from Victoria Cave, excavated in 1870. The tip is broken.

Seeds, roots, nuts and berries would have been gathered to supplement meat provided by these large herbivores and by smaller mammals, birds and fish. The small numbers of Palaeolithic hunter-gatherers meant that they did not have a major effect on the landscape although locally they may have helped concentrate the impact of the larger herbivores, particularly by reducing the numbers of large meat-eating competitors. The bones of animals such as red deer, horse and reindeer found in some caves may be remnants of human hunting expeditions but they could be the remains of meals of predators as bones of bear, lynx and fox have also been discovered.

Finds of stone implements show the development of human technology. By the post-glacial, but pre-agricultural, Mesolithic period (10,000 – 4,000 BC) the tool kit included a wide range of smaller flint and chert points and blades. Flint, unlike chert, does not occur naturally in the Yorkshire Dales: the nearest sources are the chalk outcrops of East Yorkshire, and glacial erratics from the Cumbrian coast. The flint must have been collected in person or arrived by trade or some other exchange mechanism. Some small flint implements, called microliths by archaeologists, can be as little as 13mm (0.5in) long and 3mm (0.12in) wide. They were used as barbs on shafts of antler, bone or wood. Hundreds of microliths, together with scrapers, blades, cores and thousands of pieces of waste from making flint and chert tools have been found in sheltered locations near Malham Tarn (**colour plate 2**). This, like other lakes and marshy areas in the Dales, would have attracted wildfowl as well as being a watering point for large animals and thus have been an important hunting ground. It is probably no coincidence that the most extensive finds of Mesolithic flints in the Dales have been around the tarn - the area's distinctive landforms would have made its location easy to remember and describe. We do not know the size of the Mesolithic population but groups may have varied during the year as individual families or small bands of perhaps fifteen to twenty members separated to exploit

different food resources or parts of their territory. Social contact would have been necessary to meet prospective breeding partners or to exchange information and materials like flint. A meeting place with a wide, readily available and predictable range of foodstuffs would have provided an ideal location. Excavations by Bradford University on Mesolithic sites near Malham Tarn have uncovered the remains of several hearths but as yet no structural evidence of campsites has been found. It is however, likely that simple wooden windbreaks, sometimes leant against convenient rock outcrops and tents covered with animal hide, grass or bark were used for shelter.

Careful recording and mapping of the flint and chert finds have enabled different concentrations of both tool type and raw material to be identified. This suggests not only that the area was utilised by different groups but also activity over several generations, albeit perhaps only on a seasonal, summer basis. Flint technology changed through the Mesolithic period. Flints found on early sites tend to be based on broad-blade characteristics, those from later sites tend to be more geometric in form. Most assemblages from upland sites, however, are dominated by microliths, indicating the importance of hunting.

The valleys would still have contained extensive marshes and moraine-dammed lakes. Concentrations of Mesolithic flints have been found around Semerwater while other concentrations of microliths have been found on higher ground, often close to springs, but rarely above 500m (1650ft). These may indicate campsites, close to or just above the tree line. Areas of relatively open grazing gave good sight lines, uninterrupted by trees, for bow and arrow hunting of the animals which provided meat as well as hides, antler and bone for tools. Some scatters of flint tools may indicate particular activities such as kill sites, butchery sites and hunting stands.

Studies of more recent hunter-gatherer societies suggest that the Mesolithic inhabitants of the Dales could have exploited a wide range of ecozones. The migratory movements of most mammals are generally consistent, and thus if the herds of large herbivores were followed on their spring migration to graze grounds above the tree line, nomadic Mesolithic bands could have revisited camps in, or near, preferred hunting grounds each year. Returning to the coastal lowlands in the autumn would enable the food supply to be supplemented by molluscs, crabs and seafish. Birds, fish and gathered foods such as nuts, berries, roots and fruits probably provided more of the daily calorie needs than hunted meat. As yet we do not know the size of the territories used by these early peoples. Instead of following the migratory mammals they may have restricted most of their activities to the catchment areas of particular rivers or lengths of river: a sheltered valley with good salmon runs and other fish could have provided a very attractive alternative winter base to the coast.

The Mesolithic bands probably modified their environment by using fire to drive animals for hunting purposes and, having noted that the large grazing animals were attracted to the browsing provided by scrub growing at the forest edge or in natural clearings, may have used fire and ringbarking to develop clearings. For most of the Mesolithic period any such clearance was counterbalanced by a climatic improvement which encouraged woodland. At its peak, some 8500 years ago, when the average annual temperature was about 2°C higher than today, there was a predominantly pine-elm-oak-lime woodland, with hazel perhaps associated with regeneration in former clearings and willow locally important in wetter valley areas. The woodland's precise composition would have varied throughout the Dales. Oak, for example, was probably slower to colonise on the limestone soils of Craven where pine and birch may have persisted.

The warmer temperature led to the ice-caps melting, an increase in rainfall and rising sea levels. Britain became an island. The extent of natural woodland, which had perhaps covered as much as 90 per cent of the Dales, began a decline which, with people playing an evermore important role, has continued to the present day.

Lakes and mires decreased in size as the creation of clearings and use of fire encouraged soil erosion and thus silting, mainly through run-off of water carrying particles of burnt soil and organic debris. Poaching and soil compaction by animal herds could also encourage erosion around watercourses, while soil degradation may have been increased by the loss of nutrients, such as calcium and phosphate, through grazing and by the leaching effect of rainwater.

Mature trees release several litres of water a day through transpiration, so woodland clearance may also have had an effect on peat growth by encouraging waterlogging. Most peat in the Yorkshire Dales is of the blanket bog kind, formed on poorly drained soils developed on millstone grit, shales or boulder clay. The most extensive deposits, often 2m (6.5ft) or more in thickness, are found on the watersheds on either side of Swaledale and Nidderdale and on the flanks of the Three Peaks. Huge quantities of peat have been cut for use as a fuel, but now many of the peat bogs are naturally eroding, occasionally exposing stumps and branches of trees.

The first farmers

The first farmers crossed the seas separating Britain from Europe some time after 5,000 BC, bringing with them their seed corn and domesticated cattle, sheep, goats and pigs, together with new types of implement such as leaf-shaped arrowheads, antler combs and pottery.

Agriculture was to become the dominant economic activity and to have a dramatic effect on the landscape, but the details of the change from the hunter-gatherer economy practised by the native population of the Dales are unclear. The grazing areas of the wild herds, whether on the higher moors between the growing peat bogs and the woodland fringe, on the limestone uplands or in lowland clearings, would have been equally attractive to the cattle, sheep and goats of the early pastoralists. We do not know whether these farmers, who no doubt also supplemented their diet by hunting and foraging, represented a wave of new settlers or immigrants or whether the new techniques and domesticated animals were adopted by the indigenous peoples. Transhumance, the summer movement of domestic stock from the lowlands to the uplands, is closely related to the migratory movements of the wild aurochs and deer. The earliest farmers may have been semi-nomadic or transhumant pastoralists and thus all that might remain of their campsites would be traces of hearths, scatters of occupation debris such as animal bones, broken, discarded pottery, flint knapping debris, scrapers and other tools and perhaps shallow stake holes for tent-like structures. The peat-covered moorlands and pastoral valleys do not provide good conditions for finding such remains. Leaf-shaped arrowheads, which replaced microliths as projectile points, are most often known from isolated finds suggesting losses during hunting.

A noticeable decline in the amount of elm pollen is consistently recorded in pollen diagrams from Craven, as well as the rest of the country, in the centuries around 3,000 BC. Other trees were also affected, so it is unlikely that the decline was solely due to a historic outbreak of Dutch Elm Disease or a similar epidemic. The elm decline was initially interpreted as the impact of early farmers clearing land and using elm leaves as winter fodder for their herds of cattle. It happened at about the same time across much of north-west Europe - which does not suggest a slow diffusion of agriculture through migration but provides support for the idea that indigenous groups rapidly adopted and developed the new farming techniques and made a more sustained attack on woodland. At three sites in Craven, Linton Mires, Eshton Tarn and White Moss, the decline was followed by increases in weeds and grassland species which suggest the presence of nearby clearances. No

field evidence for Neolithic cereal cultivation has been identified in the Dales although pollen analysis from Wensleydale suggests agricultural activity, mainly pastoral but also arable, around Thornton Mire.

The axes of the early farmers were made either of hard volcanic rocks, with cutting edges formed by grinding and polishing rather than flaking, or of flint. Although axes are often considered as a primary tool for forest clearance, a combination of killing trees by ringbarking followed by burning and grazing to prevent regeneration would have been more efficient. Axes would, however, be necessary for woodworking and constructing the walls and roofs of any timber buildings. The remains of two rectangular timber houses of Neolithic date, associated with large freestanding posts and pits with cultural debris, have recently been excavated at Lismore Fields near Buxton in the Peak District, but similar sites have yet to be identified in the Dales.

Long-distance contact or trade is indicated by the distribution of different types of stone axes. Thin sections cut from an axe can be examined under a microscope to enable the minerals present to be identified and matched with samples from a known quarry source. The largest group of axes found in Yorkshire originates from the central Lake District. To reach eastern Yorkshire they must have passed through the Pennines, possibly through the Stainmore gap to the north or through Craven, with flint perhaps moving in exchange. Most of the Cumbrian axes found in the Dales have been in the Ribblesdale and Aire valleys, the easiest route through Craven. Some may not have been casual losses but may have had a ritual significance, either related to the axe or the place where it was deposited.

A more settled lifestyle requires enclosures to protect stock and it is possible that some of the earth and stone banked enclosures found on the moorlands today may be Neolithic. The circular enclosure on Calverside Moor predates the overlying boundaries (**10**) while a large irregular

example on Kidstones Scar is similar to one in Teesdale where a polished stone axe was excavated. Another enclosure of possible Neolithic date lies on the summit of Rough Haw. The massive rubble stone rampart, incorporating a gritstone outcrop is carefully built but poorly sited for settlement and defence. It commands extensive views, suggesting a possible ritual purpose. Further survey and scientific excavation, however, is needed to confirm such possibilities.

During the Later Neolithic period more distinctive monuments were constructed. The circular earth-banked enclosures known as henges at Castle Dykes, near Aysgarth, and Yarnbury, near Grassington, hint at some social

10 A sheep track bisects this circular enclosure on Calverside. The low stone walls of the enclosure are overlain by a wall belonging to one of the two co-axial wall systems which subdivide the moor. Traces of the second co-axial field system can be seen north of the track in the top left corner of the photograph.

and political organisation capable of long-term planning and indicate an economy sufficiently in surplus to permit non-productive manual work over a long period. This perhaps reflects the stability of smaller territories occupied by people practising a farming economy. The Castle Dykes henge (**11**), prominently sited on a low glacial ridge, is the more impressive of the two,

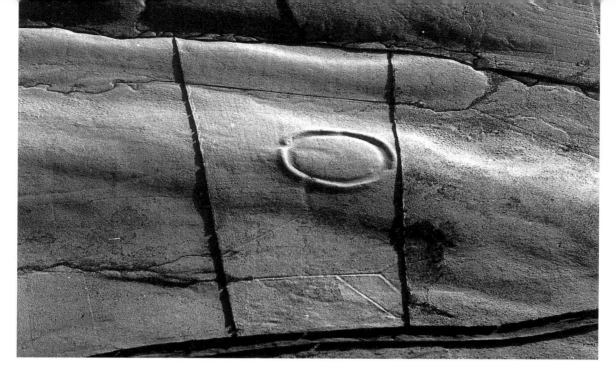

11 The Castle Dykes henge probably had a religious, economic or social purpose, where prospective partners could meet and trade resources such as stone tools. The external bank and internal ditch mean that a defensive function was unlikely.

although it is small when compared to the Thornborough Rings and other henges clustered further down the River Ure near Ripon. Castle Dykes is slightly oval, with a maximum diameter of c.75m (245ft) between the centres of the external bank which is about 9m (29ft) wide and 1.2m (4ft) high. Despite infilling by weathering over the centuries the internal ditch is still 10.5m (34ft) wide and just over one metre (3.3ft) deep. The original entrance was on the east where there is a narrow causeway across the ditch. The interior is level and gives no hint of the activities which may have taken place there.

The size, shape and position of these two henges suggest they were built in grassland rather than woodland environments. Part of the Yarnbury henge has been excavated but as this was before palaeoenvironmental sampling and analysis of soil deposits became routine it added little to our understanding of what the local environment was like before and during the construction of the monument. Pollen analysis from elsewhere in the region, however, shows a continuing, though slow, decline in the tree cover with a corresponding increase in grassland and, on some higher ground, of blanket bog.

Dead and buried?

No bodies of the earliest prehistoric inhabitants have been found, perhaps because corpses were left exposed to the attentions of carrion scavengers, a process known as excarnation. This is known for later periods elsewhere in England, as disarticulated bones have been found in the chambers of Neolithic collective tombs. These tombs, as well as providing burial places for some members of the small farming groups and thus ritual links with their ancestors, perhaps also served as territorial markers and even meeting places. Giants Grave, at the head of Pen-y-Ghent Gill, may be the remains of a chambered cairn. The site has been badly damaged but traces of at least two stone cists or chambers which contained skeletons were recorded in 1805. The remains of these chambers can still be recognised, surrounded by a circular earth bank.

It is possible that the Druid's Altar, Bordley, is the heavily robbed remains of another chambered tomb.

The use of caves as ready-made burial places and gateways to the underworld may have provided an alternative to the construction of tombs, both in the Neolithic and the succeeding Early Bronze Age. Burials are known from fifteen caves in Craven. Although none were scientifically excavated by modern standards and the records for most are poor, associated pottery and other finds suggest that at least seven caves were used for burial in the Neolithic period. A variety of burial practices is suggested by the cave finds. Disarticulated, burnt bones were found at Foxholes Cave, while at Elbolton, four articulated skeletons were found enclosed by a 'semi-circular wall of rude masonry' about 11m (40ft) from the surface. At Dowkerbottom Hole a small grave for an infant had been dug. Disarticulated and scattered bones have been recorded but this may be a result of later disturbance or the conditions of discovery.

The finds from Ravenscar Cave, excavated in the 1970s, include hearths, animal remains, pottery sherds, flint implements and a scattering of human bone. Two bodies were interred in one grave while another, towards the back of the cave, included the partial remains of two bodies with Beaker pottery, perhaps dating from the end of the third millennium BC. The cave seems then to have been deliberately blocked by two large limestone blocks in a similar manner to that of the passages of some chambered tombs, presumably to seal it and prevent further disturbance or future use as a tomb. It was, however, reoccupied, around the fourteenth-century BC, by a group who removed most of the human bone but left fragments of collared urn pottery, flint tools and a bone whistle.

More recent discoveries have come from Thaw Head Cave, Ingleton, where potholers seeking access to a deep cave system, unearthed remains of at least three people, including an adult woman and a child, together with a flint scraper and knife, a bronze pin and over 1,250

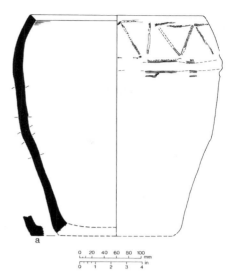

12 A cordoned barrel urn from Thaw Head Cave, drawn by J Gilks from the surviving fragments.

sherds of pottery. These included most of a later Neolithic grooved ware pot, an Early Bronze Age barrel urn (**12**) and a Later Bronze Age vessel and pieces of at least two other pots. Animal bones included roe and red deer, domestic cattle and sheep and possibly pig. These finds suggest activity on an irregular basis between c.2100 -1000 BC.

Many of the finds from earlier cave investigations still exist. Most of the pottery that has been found is so-called Peterborough ware, made in a thick, gritty dark grey or brown fabric and decorated with impressions made with twisted cord or the articulated ends of bird or small mammal bone. Other probably contemporary artifacts include leaf-shaped arrowheads, axes and bone needles. Interpretation is difficult but the hearths, pottery, animal bone and stone tools as well as human bone suggest that certain caves and overhanging rocks or rock shelters were used, perhaps intermittently over long periods, by Neolithic and Bronze Age settlers for both burial and shelter.

In the Early Bronze Age a change in burial rites took place, from the collective inhumation

13 Stoney Raise cairn, Greenber Edge. The wall between Thornton Rust and Bainbridge townships changes direction on top of the Stoney Raise cairn. Despite the removal of stone for wall building this is still 2.4m (9ft) high. Snow has blown off the more prominent walls of a series of irregular enclosures of probable early medieval date, to the east.

and cremation burials practised during the Neolithic to generally single inhumation burials crouched in flat graves or pits beneath barrows. Barrows are more common than appears at first, particularly in the southern part of the Dales where there are three main forms: earthen bowl barrows with mounds made of earth and turf; cairns with central mounds made mainly of stones; and ring cairns where there are no central mounds but a circular bank of stones and turf. Many, especially smaller ones, no doubt still await discovery but several were investigated by antiquarians and others during the nineteenth-century heyday of barrow digging as a fashionable intellectual pursuit. Occasionally barrow digger's trenches can still be recognised, as in the barrow by the Maiden Castle avenue in Swaledale, but most finds have been lost or, at best, survive with little if any associated information in museums and private collections. A few nineteenth-century excavators were more responsible and thus we know that the ditched

bowl barrow near Scale House, Rylstone, contained a burial, wrapped in woollen cloth, in an oak coffin. Fragments of the coffin and cloth survive at the Craven Museum in Skipton.

The Upper Wharfedale Exploration Society excavated three barrows above Grassington. These are sited within an extensive field system, much of which is later, where subsequent fieldwalking and the collection and recording of surface finds disturbed by moles and rabbits has revealed both leaf-shaped and barbed-and-tanged arrowheads, sherds of possible Neolithic pottery and fragments of broken stone axes. The plateau above Giggleswick, between the Aire and the Ribble valleys, contains a similar density of cairns, including a large ring cairn with a clearly defined central grave.

Some cairns were used in later periods as boundary markers, perhaps reflecting or continuing one of their original functions, but many others were attractive sources of ready assembled stone for later builders of dry stone field walls and thus have been quarried away leaving few traces of their existence. Some cairns, however, were too large to be totally obliterated. The township boundary wall between Thornton Rust and Bainbridge runs over the top of the Stoney Raise cairn. Charles Fothergill's diary of his travels in 1805 records that upwards of a thousand loads of stone had been led away from Stone(y) Raise and that it had been searched for treasure some 50 years earlier. The only finds were a few teeth in a chamber near the base of the mound. It still survives as a high stone mound, surrounded by a low stone kerb 34.5m (113ft) in diameter. Fothergill may have been exaggerating, but the evidence for stone robbing is clearly visible on the Bainbridge side of the boundary wall (**13**).

Much of a slightly smaller cairn at Sleights Pasture, Ingleton has been removed for wall building, lime burning or as rockery stone, but when dug into about 1800 it supposedly contained a stone coffin and an entire human skeleton. Three banks of stone radiate from the south side of this cairn but whether these formed part of the original monument or are a result of disturbance or subsequent use as a sheep shelter is not clear.

Many barrows and cairns are prominently sited on hilltops or false skylines. The bowl barrow above Cray, for example, has a commanding position overlooking Upper Wharfedale. An exception is the beckside position of the quaintly named Apron Full of Stones. Part of this cairn was robbed when Kingsdale Beck was straightened in the 1820's. The very active stream subsequently caused severe erosion to the cairn. This erosion was halted in 1993 by building a large retaining wall. Excavation by Alan King in 1972 revealed an empty grave, a cremation burial, a pit and a scatter of worked and waste flints. This is the only Bronze Age burial mound to have been excavated in modern times in the Dales.

Yockenthwaite, the best-known stone circle in the area, has a similar beckside position. It is possible, however, that this is not a true stone circle but an unusual stock enclosure or even a fake. Most of the stone circles in the area are small and have no obvious astronomical significance. It is likely that many originally had a burial function. One such is the embanked stone circle on Harkerside Moor, labelled on some maps as a hut circle! A better known example is the 'Druid's Altar' at Bordley. Three upright stones and the tip of a fourth survive, set centrally on a turf-covered earth and stone mound. This is about 1m (3.3ft) high and may originally have been about 12m (40ft) in diameter (**14**).

By contrast the stone circle at Mudbeck stands in a prominent position at the head of a pass in Arkengarthdale, intervisible with the Rey Cross standing stone on Stainmore.

The burial cairn at the summit of Addlebrough, is surrounded by a kerb of large gritstone boulders. Four boulders are covered in shallow cup marks but apart from one cup stone further east on Addlebrough there are no other known rock carvings in Wensleydale. There are two concentrations of carved rocks in the Dales: around the military ranges on Feldom and on the moors south of the Pateley Bridge - Appletreewick road. The latter is an outlier of the extensive

14 The Druid's Altar, Bordley. Opinions are divided as to whether this is the remains of a chambered tomb or a type of stone circle known as a four-poster.

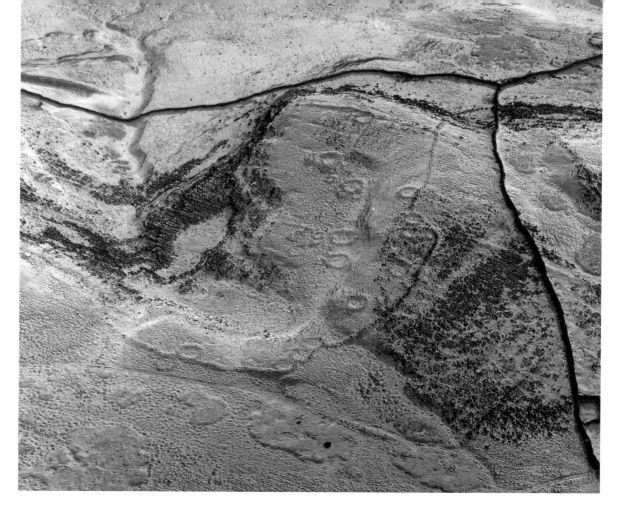

15 This group of fifteen hut circles is partly surrounded by a contemporary wall which in places overlies limestone pavement. A sheepfold nestles against one of the later enclosure walls.

group of carvings on Ilkley and Rombalds Moors in West Yorkshire. Rock carvings have been identified on over sixty earthfast boulders in the Gayles Moor area. These range from simple cups to complex patterns of cups with multiple rings and grooves (**colour plate 3**). Most known rock carvings are still *in situ* but some can be found incorporated into walls like the one over the rebuilt How Tallon cairn. Carvings are only found on sandstone boulders, no doubt because of the enduring nature and resistance to erosion of these rocks. We have no way of knowing to what extent these landscape markers were accompanied by carvings on trees which have long since decayed, or of really understanding why they exist in some areas and not apparently in other locations where similar rocks were available.

Wealth is suggested by the high quality of the Bronze metalwork from the area. Some pieces of metalwork have been discovered as a result of cairn removal but others, found in or close to streams or lakes, such as a spearhead from Semerwater, may represent ritual deposits. Two bronze axes from Reeth, apparently found with others before 1861, and the spearhead and socketed axe found at Agglethorpe in 1848 probably represent parts of hoards. The metalwork hints at the development of a social elite, possibly the same people who were buried in the barrows and cairns. However the main tools, used for every day purposes rather than prestige, continued to be of stone. The blade-based flint tools used in the early Neolithic period were replaced by cruder flake-based flint working although some finely made pressure-flaked knives, scrapers and arrowheads can be distinguished from more utilitarian tools.

Later prehistoric fields and settlements

While bowl barrows, cairns and stone circles provide direct evidence of human presence in the Dales, they give few clues as to the size of the population or to the economy and food supply or even the seasonal duration of occupation. As in later centuries the drier valley sides and lower plateaus would have been the most attractive settlement areas with the greatest economic potential. Many valley bottoms were still poorly drained marshland while the uplands were predominantly hunting and grazing areas.

Not all cairns are burial monuments. Some, especially those grouped together and associated with the remains of low banks, fields and lynchets, are clearance cairns. These are piles of stones thrown together during land clearance, sometimes against larger boulders or trees whose decay has since left a central hollow. Stone clearance, particularly where erosion was gradually removing the topsoil created by centuries of undisturbed woodland and grassland, would have been necessary to continue arable farming and would have assisted harvesting grass crops for winter stock fodder, but by its nature is very difficult to date. Most clearance cairns are found just outside the area presently enclosed by field walls, representing former agricultural use of what is now less favoured land. It is likely that many more cairns in the enclosed pastures were later cleared to make mowing with scythes easier. Few cairnfields have been found close to dateable settlements but one of the more extensive groups can be seen within a group of co-axial boundaries in the unenclosed moorland east of

Maiden Castle. A similar clearance process is apparent on some narrow limestone benches where stone has been moved to the foot of the scree slopes on each terrace.

Few settlement sites or field systems can be firmly dated. Over 700 hut circles have been mapped in the Dales, many on the limestone areas of Craven where stone structures are clearly visible on aerial photographs (15). These range from isolated hut circles to groups of fifteen or more. A few have stone walls surviving to more than a metre above floor levels, while others were simply foundations for timber superstructures. Eighty-five per cent have diameters between 3 and 8m (10 - 26ft). Not all will have been dwellings: some would have been used for workshops, storage or as animal shelters. Locations vary: some hut circles are on valley sides, others on plateau tops, while a third group occupy narrow limestone terraces. One isolated hut, at the north end of a small limestone terrace near Comb Scar, Malham, excavated in 1959, produced Bronze Age pottery, together with a few fragments of flint. The faced boulder walls were some 1.5m (5-6ft) thick and enclosed a sub-circular area about 5.5m (18ft) in diameter with a central post hole.

The group of fourteen hut circles on Burton Moor, each set within or incorporated into the walls of a series of curvilinear enclosures, which possibly functioned as garden plots or small paddocks, may be Bronze Age in date (16). The settlement lies at 450m (1500 feet) above sea level and there are no fields directly associated with it. This might suggest a pastoral or even forest economy, but a group of co-axial field boundaries and an associated trackway have recently been identified at a slightly lower altitude some 450m to the north.

The distribution and location of hut circle settlements suggest that most of them were small farmsteads, perhaps home to groups of two or three families. However, it is dangerous to infer too much about settlements just from their shape and position. During later prehistory the lower valleys in particular would have had more

16 The plan of this settlement on Burton Moor, here seen under light snow, suggests that most of the enclosures and hut circles were added, honeycomb fashion, onto a central nucleus. To the left of the main enclosures are some shallow shake holes.

extensive timber resources. Wooden buildings, which would leave fewer surface traces than stone structures and perhaps little more than a levelled platform, may have been more common, either as predecessors to stone hut circles or as independent buildings. Bedding trenches and post holes of sub-circular timber dwellings were found during excavation at Horse Close, Skipton. On higher ground stone buildings may have been extensively robbed by later wall builders.

Most hut circle settlements, whether enclosed or unenclosed, have been ascribed an Iron Age - Romano-British date, mainly as a result of small quantities of pottery found during a series of small scale excavations by Arthur Raistrick. It is dangerous to rely on largely unstratified finds for dating: the Romano-British pottery may have come from later reoccupation of sites while earlier pottery may have been less well-made

and have perished in the often acidic soils.

Scatters of flint tools and barbed and tanged arrowheads have been found in molehills in extensive prehistoric field systems such as that at Grassington, usually dated to the late first millennium BC, which have within them Bronze Age burial mounds. It is possible that these cairns were a nucleus for Bronze Age clearance and that the later field systems include and mask features formed by earlier agricultural activity.

In the southern Dales pollen analysis suggests that woodland clearance in the Bronze Age was less intense than in the preceding Neolithic or the subsequent Iron Age but work in Upper Wensleydale shows two main phases of Bronze Age agricultural activity. Both were predominantly pastoral but with more cereal cultivation than in the Neolithic, especially in the Later Bronze Age. There was a further expansion of open ground in the Iron Age.

Aerial photography, and field survey by the Swaledale Ancient Land Boundaries Project led by Andrew Fleming and Tim Laurie, have revealed the extensive remains of prehistoric field systems in mid-Swaledale (**see 10**). The remains are best preserved on the moorland on the north side of the valley where two distinct overlapping systems can be identified. Both have broad, low, parallel walls which run up to a similar cross wall. The walls were originally roughly faced and possibly topped by hedges. They enclosed large areas, extending for over a kilometre from the present moorland boundary, on what are now peat-covered acid loam soils which provide relatively poor grazing. The parallel nature and similar spacing of the walls suggest that they were laid out in an open, treeless landscape. The more fragmentary earlier system perhaps dates from the Later Bronze Age-Early Iron Age and had apparently been abandoned before the later system was built around 300 BC. The purpose of these co-axial boundaries is unclear but they perhaps defined grassland areas for winter stock management, between the more fertile lower dale sides and the higher, open, grazing lands.

Similar, though generally less well preserved patterns of co-axial field boundaries can be found elsewhere in the dales, in Wensleydale, Ribblesdale, Littondale and Wharfedale. As in Swaledale, the alignments often continue in the present day enclosures on the lower valley sides.

Six separate groups of co-axial field systems between Kettlewell and Grassington in Wharfedale have been mapped from aerial photographs. The main boundaries are spaced 30-96m (100-315ft) apart. Occasionally closer-spaced boundaries are found, probably representing droveways although these may be later insertions into the systems. They rise from the edge of the land ploughed during the medieval period, across a series of limestone benches and scars, onto the limestone plateau. It is not clear whether they ever extended onto the valley floor. One of the better-preserved

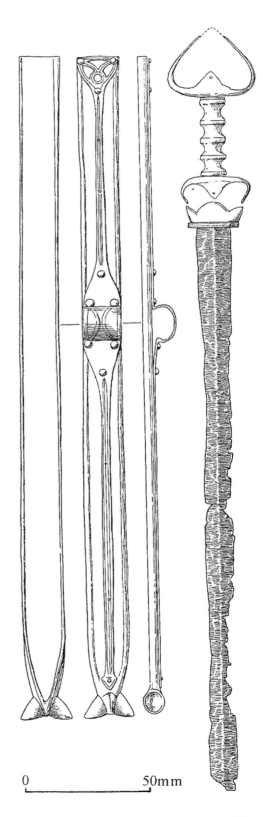

17 This long iron sword with bronze hilt fittings and sheet bronze scabbard of 'Brigantian' type, found near Cotterdale, was a symbol of high status as well as a weapon.

0   50mm

18 Ingleborough hillfort. The remains of the rampart and the 20 hut circles are very vulnerable to human disturbance, especially the removal of stones to build walker's cairns and shelters. The fragile vegetation and soil cover have been destroyed along the paths leading to the summit.

boundaries is aligned on an Early Bronze Age bowl barrow.

One block, above Grassington, which still covers over 60 hectares (145 acres) appears to have been later modified into a series of smaller fields, some nearly square, others rectangular (**colour plate 4**). A number of curvilinear enclosures within this system may represent farmsteads while part was probably further modified in the early medieval period when the Cove area was occupied by a group of farms. Some of these fields would have been used for growing spelt wheat and barley but animal husbandry probably continued as the mainstay of the economy.

It is harder to identify settlements that are definitely associated with the co-axial field systems. Circular and ovoid building platforms can be found in Swaledale in unenclosed groups or as individual platforms terraced into the hillside. Occasionally they are found within small enclosures although sometimes, as at Healaugh where the buildings were set into a pre-existing field, this may be more by chance than from an intention to provide security.

Tim Laurie has, almost singlehandedly, identified over seventy burnt mounds in Swaledale and Wensleydale. These mounds, which range in diameter from c.4 to c.15m (12 - 50ft) are composed mainly of reddened fire-cracked stones and are associated with bowl-like depressions. They are generally located near small streams, often within 50m (55yd) of the springhead and sited on open ground with a wide aspect. The volume of stone in the largest sites suggests the mounds accrued through repeated use of a site over many years.

Conventionally burnt mounds have been interpreted as cooking places, the hollows being the site of a trough or troughs in which water was brought to a boil by means of heated stones pushed down from hearths situated on the mounds themselves. An alternative explanation is that they were sweat houses - a form of sauna - the steam being contained in a tent set over the trough. Both explanations are possible and have good ethnographic parallels. As yet none have been directly linked to settlement sites.

Hillforts

The mild climate of the second millennium BC came to an end about 1250-1000 BC. Conditions deteriorated sharply and mean temperatures may have fallen by as much as 2°C. Shorter summers and longer winters not only reduced the growing season by about five weeks but, given the link between temperature and altitude, lowered the limit of crop ripening by perhaps 150m (500ft). This led to a general impoverishment of the population and an increase in mutual aggression and perhaps to a political structure based on tribal groupings with small farming communities banding together under the 'protection' of a warrior elite. The finding of a long iron sword with bronze hilt fittings and a sheet bronze scabbard, now in the British Museum, on moorland in Cotterdale west of Hawes perhaps attests to the presence of such an elite (**17**). The place name Sword Hole, mapped in 1856, suggests a possible find spot. Another bronze scabbard and sword was found on Flasby Fell. Greater emphasis on land ownership and territories is reflected in the increase in the number of defensive settlements and refuges built in the first millennium BC. Within the Dales, hillforts were probably intended as refuges during sudden raids by neighbouring groups rather than to withstand prolonged sieges.

Ingleborough dominates the lowlands to the west of the Dales (**18**). At 732m (2,350 feet) above sea level, it has long been thought of as the highest hillfort in England. Part of the plateau top is surrounded by the remains of a stone rampart. Sections have now eroded away or been disturbed by visitors building small cairns or shelters and it is not possible to positively identify an original entrance to the enclosure. On the plateau are the remains of at least twenty circular or part circular features between 5 and 8m in diameter, some nearly invisible due to erosion. Until recently these were interpreted as hut circles which implies some form of occupation. The exposed position and the absence of a good water supply for stock and humans within the enclosure argues against permanent habitation although Ingleborough would have been nearly impregnable as a short term refuge. Geophysical survey however has failed to reveal any trace of hearths within these circles. An alternative explanation is that the features are not the remains of Iron Age huts but are ring cairns, burial monuments of an earlier Bronze Age date, suggesting that Ingleborough is not a hillfort but a ritual centre.

The recently identified hillfort of How Hill, Downholme occupies a much lower, but strategic position, commanding both the Walburn gap and access to Upper Swaledale (**19**). Maiden Castle, further up the valley on the south side of Swaledale is more enigmatic (**colour plate 5**) This large hillside enclosure is surrounded by a 2 - 4m (4 - 13ft) deep external ditch and an internal bank. There are traces of a possible rampart wall on top of the bank. This would have been necessary for use of the site for defensive purposes as it is overlooked by higher ground immediately to the south. Even with a rampart any attackers may have easily controlled the interior. There is a single entrance on the east where large, roughly dressed, sandstone blocks hint at a possible gateway or gatehouse. The stone bases of two round houses lie just inside the entrance, but apart from two possible platforms for timber buildings no other features can be clearly identified inside the enclosure. The entrance is approached by a 100m (110ft) long, 5m (16ft) wide avenue,

19 The remains of the bank and ditch of the How Hill hillfort are clearly visible on the steeper, west side and, although ploughed during the medieval period, the line of the ramparts is partly fossilised in the ridge and furrow and lynchets which cover the rest of the hill.

formed by the fallen remains of two parallel stone walls, which appears to postdate the enclosure. These start just to the south of a large bowl barrow. The walls become slighter towards the east, possibly due to later robbing of stone for field walls. The purpose of the avenue is unknown: it could have been of only limited use for driving stock as the walls do not form a funnel, and is perhaps best explained as a high status entrance to the enclosure.

Maiden Castle's defensive weakness contrasts with the strong position of Castle Steads, a promontory fort overlooking Teesdale. This is defended on three sides by steep ravines and on the south by an outer bank and ditch. No hillforts are known in the southern Dales but a group of smaller defended hilltop enclosures has been identified. The most prominent examples are at Grinton (**20**) and How Hill, Low Whita in Swaledale, where areas of up to 150sq metres (165sq yds) are defended by banks and ditches, and a near-circular enclosure at Park Hill, Airton. These possibly date to the early part of the first millennium BC.

Upland areas like the Dales are frequently thought of as being marginal areas for settlement and economic activity. The upper valleys were certainly marginal in terms of arable cultivation but may have been particularly attractive to communities practising more specialist economies. The extensive grazing areas would have been attractive to pastoral communities practising transhumance, while the mineral resources, particularly copper, iron and lead, provided the basis for specialist activities. A quern production site utilising gritstone erratics

has been recognised at Helwith Bridge. It is likely that many of the millstone grit querns found elsewhere in North Yorkshire came from, as yet unidentified, quarries and outcrops in the Dales. Some sources are hinted at by placenames such as Whernside.

The main problem with trying to understand prehistoric settlement and land use in the Dales is the lack of reliable dating evidence and excavated sites. Numerous settlements and very extensive field systems have been identified in most of the dales but only the settlements at Healaugh and Gordale, which span the transition to the Romano-British period, have been excavated in recent years.

It is likely, however, that mixed farming enjoyed a long and probably uninterrupted existence in the Dales, and that the Romans found a landscape which was used by farmers who lived in a range of settlements in the lower valleys and on more favoured soils and who practised a subsistence level economy. Most

20 A ditched enclosure surrounds the top of a small moraine beside the River Swale at Grinton. A light snow cover highlights traces of ridge and furrow in the surrounding meadows.

probably occupied the same sorts of timber and stone round houses as their ancestors had for centuries, consumed grain grown in fields marked out by stone banks and hedges, corralled their stock of cattle, sheep, goats and pigs in adjacent yards, grazed them in territories recognised by their neighbours, and paid tribute in kind to a tribal elite.

3
THE ROMAN INTERLUDE: RESPONSES TO IMPERIALISM

In AD 43, when the Emperor Claudius invaded Britain, the Yorkshire Dales were under the control of the Brigantian Queen Cartimandua and her consort Venutius. The frontier arrangements made by the first Roman Governor of Britain suggest that Cartimandua soon decided to ally herself to Rome. This enabled the Romans to subdue southern Britain without fear of interference from the north but not all of the tribes which formed the Brigantian confederacy may have agreed with her policy.

In AD 52 Cartimandua handed over the Catavellaunian leader, Caratacus, who had sought refuge in Brigantia. Although she was rewarded with gifts by the Romans, this betrayal of a kinsman helped create a rift between Cartimandua and some of her peoples. In AD 69 she brought matters to a head by divorcing Venutius who, aware of the brutal Roman subjugation of Wales and southern England, then moved to take-over the Brigantian confederacy. Cartimandua was eventually rescued by Roman auxiliaries, leaving Venutius in control of Brigantia and the Romans with a hostile neighbour on their northern border. It is possible that the hoard of bronzes from decorated cavalry harness, found at Fremington in Swaledale and now in the British and Yorkshire Museums, represents loot hidden by one of Venutius' followers during these upheavals (**21**).

Camps and Forts

Petilius Cerialis, appointed Governor of Britain in AD 71, had the task of conquering the Brigantes. The legionary size (8.2ha, 20.25 acres) marching camp on Malham Moor (**22**) may date from Cerialis' campaign. Its *claviculae*, the curved internal extension of the banks, which guard the entrances to the camp, suggest that it is of first-century date. Such slight structures, built by the army as a temporary overnight base when on campaign, can be destroyed easily by ploughing, and as yet no similar camps within a day's march (20km; 12 miles) in any direction have been identified. The Malham camp lies on a relatively flat plateau, probably already largely treeless by the first century AD, which would have been more suited to the manoeuvring of a large force than many of the narrow, steep-sided valleys in the Dales. It is bisected by Mastiles Lane, a relatively easy route between the Ribble and Wharfe valleys. This green lane is often thought to be medieval but may well be of Roman or earlier origin.

Other marching camps at Catterick and across the Stainmore gap are evidence of the Roman offensive. It is likely that the Brigantes operated a guerilla-type campaign and that Cerialis attempted to destroy the economic base for any resistance. The major earthworks north of the Dales at Stanwick, close to the trans-Pennine route over Stainmore, were once thought to be a hillfort hastily erected by Venutius in advance of the Roman armies. Recent excavations, however, show that the

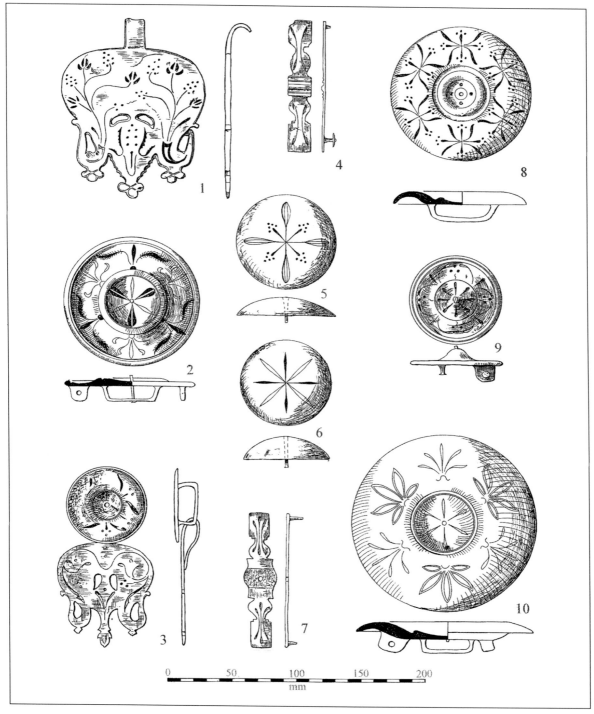

21 Some of the bronze pendants (1,3), decorative strips (4, 7) and roundels from a hoard of Roman cavalry horse harness found at Fremington in the early nineteenth century.

22 This large marching camp on Malham Moor probably dates from the initial conquest of the Dales in the first century AD. Earthworks such as this were erected by the Roman army at each camping place, even for a single overnight stop, when on campaign or manoeuvres. Mastiles Lane follows the field wall across the centre of the camp.

23 Light snow picks out the position of old excavation trenches and spoil heaps as well as the defences of the Bainbridge fort and its eastern annexe.

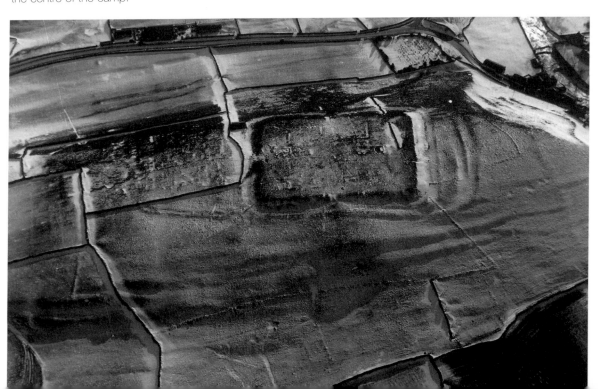

main defensive earthworks had been constructed within a relatively short period around the middle of the first century AD and that associated settlement remains, with high quality imported pottery and other finds, cover several hectares. This suggests that Stanwick had been the centre of the pro-Roman client kingdom.

The plough-flattened remains of a fort at Wensley (**colour plate 6**), sited on a low-lying gravel terrace close to the River Ure, were only discovered through aerial photography in 1976. It has never been excavated but may date from the first century when the Dales, like the rest of the Pennine uplands, were ringed by forts and military roads, to aid control of the native population. Excavations at the forts at Elslack, Ilkley, Bowes, Brough under Stainmore and Catterick have all produced evidence for occupation during the Agricolan period (AD 78-85) and it is likely that the forts at Burrow in Lonsdale (Overborough) and Low Borrow Bridge were also occupied.

Near the centre of the Dales is the fort at Bainbridge, extensively, though by no means completely, excavated between 1925 and 1969 (**23**). It occupies a hog-backed glacial mound, truncated on the west by the River Bain, and probably began as an Agricolan guardpost. The defences of this phase have not been identified, but the oldest buildings so far discovered are obliquely aligned to the remains of the later fort, first built c. AD 90-105. It remained occupied, except perhaps for a period between c. AD 120 and 160, until the end of the Roman period in the early fifth century.

The fort measures about 91 by 111m (300 by 365ft) between the crests of the ramparts and has an interior area of about 1ha (2.5 acres). The ramparts are parallel but each corner is about 6o out from a right angle, probably a result of a deliberate attempt to maximise the site's defensive capabilities. Excavations of the defences revealed a clay rampart, later strengthened by a sandstone face and revetment. In the north-west corner this bank still survives to nearly 4m (13ft). The main ditches outside the rampart are now largely silted up but were up to 5.2m (16.5ft) wide and of typical V-shaped section. Their number varies according to the lie of the ground: two on the north, one on the south and as many as five on the west. Here, excavation showed that the four outer ditches, all of similar size and shape, had been deliberately backfilled, suggesting that they had been a short-lived response to a perceived threat.

There were four gateways although the west gate, now marked by a small break in the rampart and a later mound in the ditch, was probably little used. The east gate, now visible as a 4.9m (16ft) wide break in the rampart, was excavated in 1926 and 1931. It was approached by a causeway across the ditch. Further excavation in 1959 suggested that it was a replacement for one further south. The north and south gates, linked by the *via principalis*, are more clearly defined but only the south and east gateways would have been usable by wheeled traffic.

The appearance of the present earthworks inside the fort owes more to the twentieth-century excavations than to the remains of Roman buildings. The course of the *via principalis* is still discernible, and excavation has revealed the presence of a typical range of buildings including a headquarters building with the commanding officer's house to the south. The headquarters building, rebuilt in the late second century, overlay part of a granary complex. The north part of the central range was also occupied by granaries. A series of early, stone-built barrack blocks was found in the south-east corner of the fort.

East of the fort is a subrectangular annexe, about 0.75ha (1.8 acres) in area, identified as the *bracchium caementicium* (stone-built outwork) built when Alfenus Senecio (AD 205-208) was Governor of the Province of Britain. This was recorded on a now lost dedication slab (**24**). A range of timber-built buildings with stone floors in the annexe were destroyed by fire during the third century and later replaced by stone buildings. For most of the third century the

24 Part of an inscribed dedication slab found at Bainbridge sometime before 1600. The inscription translates as "For the Emperor Caesar Lucius Septimius Severus Pius Pertinax Augustus and for the Emperor Caesar Marcus Aurelius Antoninus Pius Felix Augustus and the Publius Septimus Geta, most noble Caesar, the Sixth Cohort of Nervians built this [rampart] of uncoursed masonry with annexe wall under the charge of Lucius Alfenus Senecio, senator of consular rank: Lucius Vivius Pius, commander of the cohort, centurion of the ... Legion ..., had direction of the work."

annexe formed an extension of the fort as the earlier east wall dividing them had been taken down, but the wall of the fort was rebuilt on its original alignment at the beginning of the fourth century. The garrison which built the extension, the Sixth Cohort of Nervii, is unlikely to have required more accommodation than was available in the fort before its extension, so the annexe was presumably for additional troops.

Civilian settlements developed around most Roman forts and Bainbridge is unlikely to have been an exception: William Camden, a sixteenth-century antiquarian, mentions 'traces of many houses' below the fort to the east. These, however, were not necessarily Romano-British in origin as at least one medieval tenement is recorded in this area. This has not been identified by excavation, most of which has concentrated on the interior of the main fort and the annexe to the east, although there are undocumented references to Roman buildings under the present day Brough Farm.

Roman Roads

The Bainbridge fort occupies a strategically strong position controlling the principal pass through the Pennines between the Stainmore and the Ilkley-Aire gaps (**25**). Much of the route of the road west of the fort towards Lancaster is well known as it rises up 230m (750ft) towards Cam Houses and Ribblehead and thence down Chapel le Dale, although the route west of Ingleton has not been traced. This is the clearest length of Roman road in the Dales, other than part of the main north-south military highway, from Manchester to the frontier at Carlisle, through the Lune Valley, parallel with the route since taken by the main West Coast railway line and the M6. This road can be clearly seen across moorland at Carlingill, near Gibbet Hill, as a 3m (10ft) wide cambered bank or 'agger'. Two Roman milestones still survive near Kirby Lonsdale and Middleton. A road through the Rawthey valley from Brough towards Sedbergh is also traceable across Bluecaster and may have linked with a yet-to-be identified fort somewhere near Sedbergh.

The fort at Bainbridge would not have been only accessible from the south-west. Two routes for a road running south towards Wharfedale and Ilkley have been suggested. One climbs in short straight lengths towards Carpley Green and thence across Stake Allotments to Stake Moss and then down a well-engineered track through Cray to Buckden; from here its course becomes uncertain but probably followed the Wharfe valley down through Barden. An alternative, but less steep route, between the fort and Stake Moss, follows the present road towards Stalling Busk and thence along another well-engineered track across Cragdale Allotments to Stake Moss.

A northerly route would have connected with the road and forts controlling the Stainmore pass, probably running up Wensleydale towards Mallerstang and thence to Brough. Another road would have run east, down Wensleydale, towards the forts at Wensley and Healam Bridge and the main Roman road up the east side of the province from Isurium (Aldborough) towards

Catterick and the north. A strategic network of military roads linking forts surrounded the Dales and enabled the rapid movement of troops. No signal stations associated with this network, such as that excavated during widening of the A66 on Bowes Moor in 1989, have been positively identified in the Dales, although possible sites have been identified along the road to the west including Gibbet Hill in the north-west corner of the National Park. This strategic road network would have been supplemented by a web of minor tracks linking the valleys and minor settlements, but only routes which met local needs would have continued in use after the Roman period.

Andrew Fleming has recently identified the route of a possible Roman road from the River Ure near Ulshaw Bridge, near Middleham, through the Walburn gap to Swaledale and the lead-mining field in the Hurst area. A pig (ingot) of lead with the inscription Hadrian was

reputedly found near Hurst prior to 1859. No trace of this pig has since been found, nor have any recognisably Roman lead workings been identified in the Swaledale-Arkengarthdale mining field or indeed elsewhere in the Dales. This is perhaps not surprising as it is extremely difficult to date mining remains from surface evidence alone and the area has been heavily worked and reworked in subsequent centuries. This route would have provided access to a navigable waterway, perhaps a simpler route for transporting lead than down the Swale valley to Catterick.

Two other lead pigs of Roman date, inscribed IMP CAES DOMITIANO AUG COS VIII found in the Hayshaw Bank area, east of Greenhow Hill in 1733-4 still survive (26), one being in the British

25 The network of Roman roads and forts surrounding the Yorkshire Dales. Many more tracks would have been used, especially for non-military purposes.

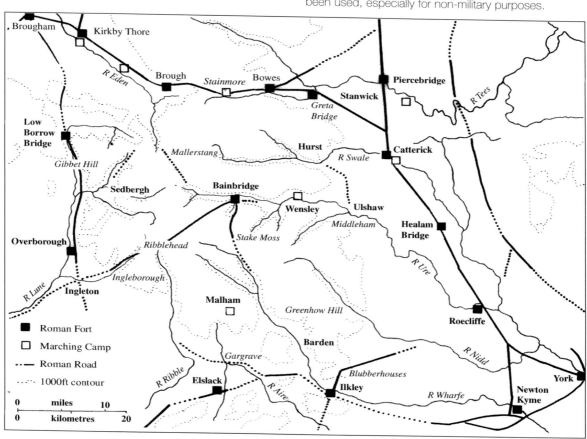

Museum. A third pig, now lost but apparently inscribed with the name of the Emperor Trajan, was found near Appletreewick. The Hayshaw Bank pigs, dating to AD 81, indicate a relatively rapid Roman exploitation of the lead industry, presumably under Imperial control, and probably organised, at least in part, through the network of forts. This suggests that the lead deposits may have been worked prior to the Roman Conquest and that lead may have been the Roman's main economic interest in the Dales. During excavation by Alan King in 1966 at Victoria Camp, above Victoria Cave, a clay-lined bowl was found, containing almost one hundredweight of barytes with traces of malachite, a copper mineral, charcoal and a small amount of slag. The clay in the lower levels of the bowl was reddened by heat which suggests that it was the remains of a small bowl furnace.

Native Settlements

Lead mining and processing was a labour-intensive industry. It is not known how densely settled the Dales were prior to the Roman Conquest, although palaeoenvironmental evidence for Swaledale, Wensleydale and the Craven area shows an increasing amount of woodland clearance and arable cultivation towards the end of the Iron Age which continued and intensified during the Roman occupation. Few settlements have been closely dated to this period, mainly due to the very limited amount of excavation and the relative lack of dateable material due to the thin, acidic nature of most soils.

One of the earliest excavations on a settlement site, in 1894, produced over 400 sherds of what the excavators, the Upper Wharfedale Exploration Society, called British and Romano-British pottery. A series of small enclosures near Park Stile in Grass Wood, Grassington was investigated over a two-month period by the Society's labourers. The finds included a single mid-fourth-century coin as well as worked antler and quern stones. The Society also dug in a settlement on Lea Green, Grassington, and reported quantities of Roman

26 One of the pair of lead pigs (ingots) found on Hayshaw Bank in 1734. It is 578mm (22.75in) long and weighs 70.3kg (155lb).

pottery and worked stone as well as 'animal bones, mainly burnt, in seventy-one of the seventy-two holes and trenches made' (**27**).

Well-recorded excavations, however, are rare. An exception is the work of Andrew Fleming and Tim Laurie in Swaledale. Part of one settlement at Healaugh was examined between 1988 and 1990. This consisted of a group of six or seven building platforms, partly scooped into the hillside. Excavation of one platform revealed remains of the stone walls of an oval house, 9 by 5m (30 by 16ft) with an entrance at the east end, and a stone paved floor (**colour plate** 7). Further excavation showed that this was a rebuild of a smaller circular building with a thick stone wall built in 'post and panel' style. This in turn had been preceded by a circular or near circular wooden building marked by a shallow ring groove. The few fragments of pottery associated with the oval building were mainly of second century AD date suggesting that this represented a rebuilding of an Iron Age settlement. The excavation of enclosure banks partly surrounding the settlement showed that it had been built within part of an earlier field system of long narrow fields whose principal boundaries ran across the contours, possibly a continuation of the co-axial fields noted on the moorland above. Several similar settlement platforms have now been recognised in comparable hill slope positions in Swaledale.

A hoard of sixty-two silver coins found by a metal detector user at Grinton in 1987, and dating from the AD 170s, is one of the few stray finds of Roman material recorded from the dale this century, although other Roman coins were apparently found near Maiden Castle in the nineteenth century.

Two sites in Littondale have received more limited attention. A D-shaped earthwork near Thornsber Barn, some 50 by 45m (165 by 148ft), stepped into three terraces and incorporating a number of smaller building platforms, was investigated in 1968. A trench, dug through one of three possible buildings, revealed a coin minted in AD 243-4 and a fragment of a mortarium on the rubble floor. The hut wall contained four other quern fragments, an iron knife and sherds of coarse pottery as well as a number of animal bones. This site was interpreted as a native farmstead (28). Recent survey by Stephen Moorhouse, however, suggests that the enclosure, which is surrounded by other earthworks, is rather more complex than the limited excavation indicated. The enclosure has been disturbed by later rectangular buildings and overlies an earlier field system. It is possible that the Roman material may relate to buildings associated with this earlier field system.

Further up the valley, a team from Manchester University excavated part of a group of small sub-rectangular enclosures at New Ing Barn, in 1992. Although no buildings were positively identified, paved and cobbled areas were exposed, together with a small quantity of pottery, quern fragments and other finds, which the excavators interpreted as a small farmstead occupied in the late third and early fourth centuries AD. A coin and the presence of pottery from the Nene valley suggested that the inhabitants were involved in a market economy and not just subsistence farming.

The pottery recovered from excavation of a group of hut circles known as Attermire Camp, recently re-examined by Sonia Allen, is the largest assemblage of Romano-British pottery from a settlement site yet studied in the Dales. The finds and the date range of the pottery suggests that the settlement was founded in the second century, was most prosperous during the third century and declined in the fourth. The collection includes Samian ware imported from France as well as more local vessels. None was in the local Iron Age tradition recorded by Raistrick on numerous other sites in the Dales.

The position for most of the other Dales is similar; there are scatters of settlement earthworks and traces of associated, sometimes very regular, field systems though few stand in isolation. As yet no other settlements have been dated by finds made during modern scientific excavation or by independent dating techniques.

Villas

There are two more formal Roman settlements, villas, on the edge of the Dales. The Gargrave villa is located on well-drained loamy clays which overlie the gravel of a former glacial lake. Like Bainbridge fort it has been subject to extensive investigation: in c.1735, c.1805, 1910 and 1973-78. Aerial photographs show that it was surrounded by an extensive ditched field system, part of which consisted of long narrow fields, the other a series of more or less squarish plots, perhaps paddocks. The field system may have covered an area of 40ha (100 acres) and been supplemented by grazing on unenclosed moorland. The earliest evidence for occupation on the site is a number of circular timber and turf-built houses. One of these survived into the villa period but was not necessarily still used as a dwelling. The packing of its last central post used box tiles from a hypocaust, the Roman form of underfloor heating.

In the second half of the second century a house with a front corridor and a central entrance between slightly projecting wings was developed. This had mosaic floors and a detached bathhouse as well as an internal bath suite. Water was supplied through iron-collared wooden pipes. Two new house buildings were subsequently added, together with a single-roomed squarish building at one time linked to one of the new houses by a covered walk.

The main part of the site was enclosed, excluding any farm buildings, possibly in the early third century. In the late third century a partly walled enclosure, identified by the excavator, Brian Hartley, as a possible stackyard, was inserted into the southwestern corner of the enclosure (**colour plate 9**). The principal early houses appear to have been abandoned, and possibly robbed, during the fourth century.

27 The settlement on Lea Green, excavated in the 1890s. The rectangular buildings suggest early medieval as well as Romano-British occupation. A later dewpond lies beside the stone walls in the foreground.

Although a new house may have been built on another part of the site the final activity seems to have been the construction of a hearth made from roof tiles from the roof of the north house. This hearth overlay fallen wall plaster and may have been used for cooking by shepherds or others sheltering in the ruins.

Although bone preservation was poor due to the acidic soils, the presence of quantities of pig bone suggests grazing on uncleared woodland. Large amounts of wood would also have been required for fuel, especially for the bathhouse and other hypocausts, as well as for building and general repair work.

The evidence for a villa at Middleham is less conclusive, but in 1881 the remains of a hypocaust were identified. The site was investigated again in 1940 when a stone-built room, heated by two cross flues and a flue running round the walls was discovered. A polished white concrete floor rested on large stones and tiles. No other buildings have yet been identified here.

The caves

The discovery of Roman coins, brooches, spindle whorls and beads in Victoria Cave in 1838 sparked off extensive investigations of cave sites in the Settle area. These reached a peak with the excavations at Victoria Cave in the 1870s, but continued into the first half of the twentieth century during which time most caves were cleared of all archeological deposits.

Fortunately many of the finds from these excavations have survived, together with diaries and other records, which are now enabling the caves to be reassessed. The finds include quantities of local and imported pottery such as Samian ware, glass bangles, beads, stone implements such as spindle whorls, antler and bone items and metalwork. The brooches have received most attention. Some fifty-seven brooches are recorded from Victoria Cave, as well as twenty-nine from Attermire Cave, ten from Kelco Cave and seven from Sewell Cave. They are of a range of types and dates, but close study of those from Victoria Cave and the high proportion of brooches in the finds from nearby caves has led to suggestions that the area may have had workshops for brooch manufacture, with a market perhaps being sought in the military garrisons or forts in the area. A small 2.25cm (0.9in) lens-shaped lead ingot from either Dowkerbottom or Victoria Cave may have come from a metallurgical crucible and thus indicate a metal-working industry.

Cut and unshaped antler, bone and horn cores as well as unfinished items, recently identified by Martin Dearne during re-examination of worked bone and other finds from Victoria Cave, indicate boneworking in the area. The so-called spoon brooches are among the most decorative items (**28**). Although they are rare elsewhere, twenty-one examples are known from Victoria Cave, which suggests that they too may have been made nearby. Some of the worked bone, especially toggles, showed signs of wear but many other pieces have little or no signs of use. Two weaving combs and a number of spindle whorls suggest cloth manufacturing, while toggles, needles and pins suggest sewing and fastening of coarse cloth or leather.

Many caves, particularly Attermire, are sited on steep scree slopes. These slopes may have been covered with trees and scrub during Roman times and are not easily accessible today. Craft working would have been difficult inside dark damp caves and is thus unlikely to have taken place within them. It is therefore possible that the caves were used as hideaways and that the finds represent chance losses. Many of the finds are higher-status objects than those recovered from investigation of local settlements. The difference is more than would be expected from just the better conditions for preservation found in caves and the sieving techniques used by their excavators to recover objects. This suggests that many finds represent offerings made during deliberate occupation of the caves, perhaps as some form of rites of passage. However, the date range of the Roman material from the caves spans most of the Roman occupation of the area and the activities may well have varied during this time. Recent examination of the pottery from Victoria Cave supports this view. Most of the early Roman material is abraded and in small

pieces, whereas the later, fourth-century material is larger and less abraded, suggesting it was broken *in situ*, possibly deliberately.

The relatively stable political regime imposed after the incorporation of Brigantia into the Roman province, notwithstanding a period of unrest in the mid-second century, provided conditions for economic prosperity. Even before the Conquest the area was extensively occupied and cultivated, albeit with a subsistence level economy. The Roman military occupation placed considerable burdens on this native economy; the high costs of transport meant that as large a proportion as possible of the foodstuffs and raw materials consumed by the garrisons would have been acquired locally, with some products exported to meet the demands of the army elsewhere. Excavations at Catterick fort, for example, discovered evidence for a large leather-working depot. Many of the hides required for this would have been delivered on the hoof from the Dales.

While it is difficult to date the extensive field systems and settlements found throughout most of the area, the limited excavation evidence on civil sites in the Dales suggests a continuation of the subsistence economy, although imported pottery and lead extraction and metal processing activities imply connection with the market economy. Nevertheless, most of the population had few material possessions and the main trappings of Roman civilisation were only apparent at more environmentally favoured locations on the fringes of the Dales.

28 A bone 'spoon brooch' excavated from Victoria Cave in 1870.

4

'WILD AND LONELY THE LAND THEY LIVE IN, WIND SWEPT RIDGES AND WOLF-RETREATS'

Just as many Iron Age settlements continued in use after the Roman occupation of the area, it is likely that settlements continued after the legions had withdrawn. Successful farmland would not have been abandoned without good reason, although political upheaval, an increase in civil unrest, the demise of the market economy, a deteriorating climate, crop failures and a corresponding increase in disease and famine, all influenced population size and location. The collapse of the Roman market economy, however, deprived archaeologists of common material, such as coins and traded pottery, which can be dated easily.

Modern research is beginning to throw a little light on the appearance of the Dales in the 'Dark Ages', the five and a half centuries between the end of the Roman occupation and the Norman Conquest, when the area was subjected to Anglian, and later Scandinavian, immigrants and influence. The sources, however, are few and varied: much is still supposition. There are no Anglo-Saxon charters - virtually no documentary sources until the Domesday Book of 1086. Only three sites which definitely fit into this period have been excavated, but to complement these there are some distinctive carved sculptures, a host of placenames, dialect terms and phrases, and some limited environmental evidence. The chapter title is a quotation from the epic poem *Beowulf.* It aptly describes the higher part of the Dales, although some of the valleys would have been more hospitable.

The political background.

The Yorkshire Dales lay on the fringes of the main chiefdoms which developed after the withdrawal of the Roman garrisons from Northern England in the late fourth and early fifth centuries. Northern England appears to have passed into the control of a series of small, independent kingdoms ruled by native British dynasties. The political geography becomes recognisable only in the late sixth century, by which time many kingdoms had fallen under the control of Anglian warlords, but was always fluid and subject to frequent, sometimes rapid, change (**29**). To the north-west lay the kingdom of Rheged, to the east lay Catraeth, perhaps best equated with Catterick, and to the south-east lay

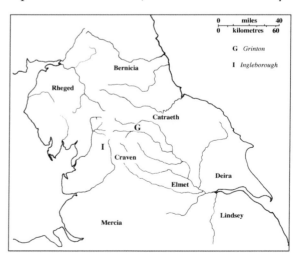

29 The position of the main kingdoms in the sixth century.

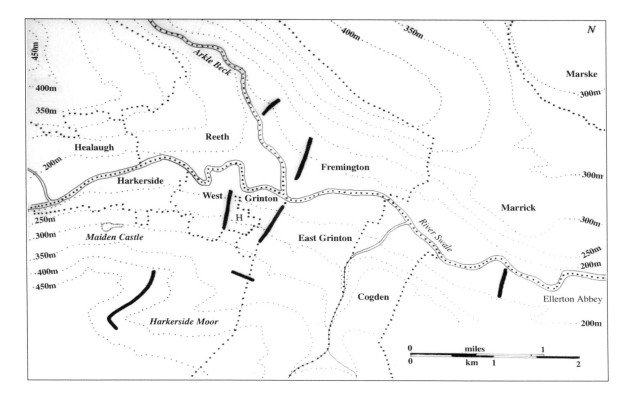

30 The earthwork dykes and later administrative divisions in and around Grinton. The absence of dykes on the floodplains of the River Swale and the Arkle Beck may be due to later erosion or, more likely, to the existence of marshy ground when the dykes were built but the pattern on Harkerside is harder to explain. The east-west dyke in particular stops very abruptly for no apparent topographic reason suggesting the network was unfinished due to changes in political circumstances. H - a detached part of Harkerside township.

the kingdom of Elmet. There seems to have been another British kingdom, based around Craven and bordering Elmet on the west, which was absorbed by the English earlier than Elmet. Craven certainly existed as an administrative unit at the time of the Norman Conquest. It is recorded in the Domesday Book as the wapentake of *Cravescire*, and later as an archdeaconry. North-east of Catraeth arose the Anglian kingdom of Bernicia.

Bernicia developed in importance and power in the late sixth century. In 603 its warrior-king, Aethelfrith, won control of Deira (eastern Yorkshire) and created a new kingdom of Northumbria. This was to dominate northern England and Southern Scotland and maintain a separate identity right up to the Norman Conquest. Within the main kingdoms there were distinct territorial units such as the regione *Dunutinga*, recorded in an early eighth-century document. Placename and tenurial evidence suggests that *Dunutinga* was centred on

Ingleborough, thus raising the possibility that it had developed from a pre-Roman, Brigantian clan or group responsible for the hillfort.

The system of large linear dykes centred on Grinton and Fremington form part of the boundary of another early, post-Roman, British polity (**30**; **31**). The core of this system consists of two linear earthworks, separated by some 500m (550yd), with ditches on their eastern sides. These are most visible in the enclosed

31 The bank of the central cross valley dyke at Grinton is topped by a stone field wall and a row of pollarded elm trees. These have since died of Dutch Elm Disease. This was one of two dykes in the Grinton System which formed part of a township boundary.

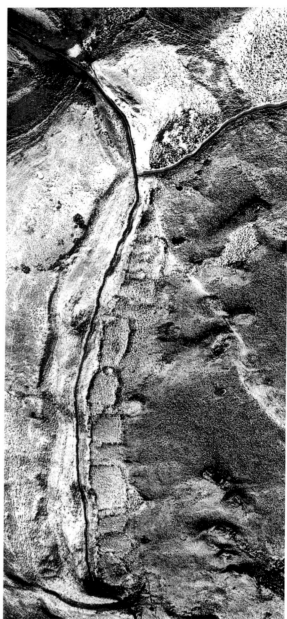

32 Tor Dyke formed part of the northeast boundary of the kingdom of Craven. It was used as a township, parish, deanery, wapentake and, until 1974, county boundary and also formed part of the boundary of the medieval Scale Park. The enclosures on the east side of the dyke have not yet been dated.

pastures on either side of the valley. One dyke extends on to the floodplain of the Swale, but neither extends on to the unenclosed moorland above the valley sides. A third, somewhat smaller, dyke lies some 2.5km (1.5 miles) to the east. On the moorland above Grinton are two other dykes, one partly surrounding the eastern flank of Harkerside, the other extending some 300m (330yd) west of the narrow gorge of Grinton Gill. The dykes appear to block access into Upper Swaledale and Arkengarthdale from the east. They have been linked with the stand by Venutius against the Romans in AD 69-74 but recent fieldwork by Andrew Fleming has shown that the western dyke slights a probable Romano-British settlement at Dykehouse Close and that the central dyke has also been built across field banks associated with other settlements of probable Iron Age - Romano-British date. One dyke runs through Fremington, dividing the township into two. The township is unlikely to have developed on both sides of a major boundary dyke if it was in use. The placename Fremington, meaning Frema's farm, mentioned in Domesday Book, probably originated between AD 750 and 950, suggesting that the Grinton-Fremington dykes are earlier, built in the fifth, sixth or perhaps early seventh centuries to mark the boundary between native and Anglian territory.

To the east of Swaledale lies the more extensive Scots Dyke, which represents another boundary between Anglian and native territories. More impressive, though shorter, is Tor Dyke, on the watershed between Wharfedale and Coverdale (32). This was also once claimed as a defensive earthwork constructed during the late Iron Age in advance of the Roman invasion, but is now believed to have been the north-eastern boundary of the kingdom of Craven.

In the late eighth century small groups of Vikings, raiders from Scandinavia, began attacking coastal communities in England. Norse colonisation followed. Northumbria was the first English kingdom to collapse, a Danish army led by Halfdan capturing York in 867. Deira was left in the hands of a client king but the army returned to Northumbria in 869 and again in 873. In 876 the *Anglo-Saxon Chronicle* records that Halfdan rewarded his followers by sharing 'out the lands of Northumbria and they were engaged in ploughing and making a living for themselves'. Halfdan's warriors are unlikely to have been directly engaged in tilling the ground. More likely they entered local society as owners of the estates of their vanquished competitors. Some peasants, however, may well have followed their leaders and been directly involved in farming while other, Irish-Norse, raiders and colonists arrived in the tenth century.

Northumbrian autonomy ended with the defeat of Eric Bloodaxe on Stainmore in 954. The former kingdom was then ruled by the West Saxon kings through appointed archbishops and earls who also had interests in the south in an attempt to break down its independence.

The carved stones

Stone carving was a hallmark of the Anglian monastic church. Although the pagan Scandinavian settlers who came to Britain had no tradition of stone carving they adopted the custom and developed it with new kinds of decoration and ornament. The difficulty of moving large pieces of stone means that sculptures were usually quarried and carved near where they have been found. Their creation appears to have depended on patronage, which makes the distribution of stone sculpture particularly useful for historians and archaeologists as it provides some information about settlement and society. Unfortunately, carvings are rarely found in dated contexts, but they partially compensate for the absence of pottery, which was little used in this period in northern England.

The earliest carved stones in the Dales have been found in Lower Wensleydale, significantly an area where Anglian placenames predominate. This wide valley was suited to arable agriculture and thus generated the wealth which supported the production of sculpture. It seems likely that Wensley was an important ecclesiastical, perhaps monastic, centre as within the later, medieval, church of Holy Trinity are two early eighth-century slabs inscribed 'Donfrid' and 'Eadberehct', several mid-to-late-eighth-century fragments, part of the upright shaft of an early tenth-century cross and the shaft of an eleventh-century cross.

A bronze pin and stylus found in Wensley churchyard of eighth- or ninth-century date are Anglian in style, but a later burial found here during grave digging was that of a Viking farmer. His skeleton, aligned east-west, was found with a two-edged iron sword with a pommel decorated with applied silver strips and panels with geometric and formalised leaf ornament, an iron knife and fragments of an iron spearhead and sickle blade. The sword is of Anglo-Saxon style of ninth- or early-tenth-century date, but the burial it accompanied was that of a pagan Viking who wanted to take his tools and weapons to Valhalla as a mark of his status. This suggests that the incoming settlers were using an existing cemetery for burial, or perhaps that the warrior was uncertain about Christianity and wanted to hedge his bets.

Other parts of crosses have been discovered further up Wensleydale: at West Witton, Aysgarth and Carperby cum Thoresby. Two glass beads, three brooches and an iron shield boss, strap end and knife, found near East Witton in 1884, are likely to be grave goods and had probably been buried in a late-pagan Anglian cemetery. They date from the early seventh century AD and provide further evidence for the Anglian advance into the Dales, which had been taking place along the main river valleys since the sixth century.

The relatively inhospitable nature of the upper valleys may be one reason why there are few examples of the distinctive recumbent grave covers known as hogbacks, which are a characteristic feature of the Viking settlement of Northern England. Although found on both sides of the Pennines only three have so far been discovered within the Dales, all at Burnsall. They are now kept within St Wilfred's Church, together with twelve tenth- or eleventh-century cross fragments, most of which were found here in the late nineteenth century. The shape and ornament of many hogbacks suggests that they are in part representations of contemporary houses or shrines, but only one of the Burnsall hogbacks has carvings of roof tiles or shingles.

The rural economy

Throughout Europe there were outbreaks of pestilence in the mid-sixth century and again in the late-seventh and early-eighth centuries. These resulted in a dramatic decline in the overall population and its age structure and led to the abandonment of many less-attractive settlements, as well as a shift in landuse away from labour intensive arable agriculture towards pastoralism. The effect on the population of the Dales is not known, but population decline may partly explain why many later placenames refer to clearings - abandoned pastures and fields will become scrub in less than a generation and return to woodland within two or three generations.

However, pollen analysis does not suggest an immediate change in landuse after AD 350, but rather a gradual shift away from arable

agriculture. The Ellerton Moor pollen diagram from Swaledale suggests that arable cultivation was at its height in about AD 320-410. After this there was a gradual increase in tree pollen, which reached its maximum extent, though not back to pre-Iron Age levels, in AD 745-865. This pattern is replicated in Nidderdale, Wensleydale and Craven. Thereafter there was a gradual decrease in tree pollen, suggesting increasing clearance of secondary woodland. This clearance may have been by incoming settlers or by a population expanding through its own resources or both, and was helped by a climatic improvement which probably included a decline in rainfall.

Placenames provide another key to understanding the rural population, although they must be treated with caution as many names have been distorted by time and transcription and it is not often clear who is responsible for the name, the native population of an area or a new wave of immigrants. Most of the Yorkshire placenames which contain the element *thveit* (eg Thwaite, Braithwaite, Blakethwaite - implying the clearing of land by the chopping down of trees) are found in the Dales. They are probably a reliable indication of settlement newly established by Vikings on vacant land, although it is possible that a name was merely transferred from Scandinavia without any consciousness of its meaning. Some 60 per cent of the placenames in the Settle-Sedbergh area are Scandinavian in origin, although the form of some suggest that they were given by people who had earlier settled in Ireland rather than by settlers coming directly from the east. Many of the Scandinavian placename elements describe the landscape. Winskill, for example, means windswept shielings, Raisgill a ravine with a cairn and Sedbergh a seat-shaped flat hill. Uldale probably indicates a valley frequented by wolves, man's only competitor amongst the local fauna. Even today the dialect of the upper Dales contains numerous words of Scandinavian origin.

Most of the vills recorded in the Domesday Book within the area of the National Park are recognisable as settlements today although the distribution of names is patchy. They suggest Norse occupation at the valley heads and marginal areas with English settlement generally in the lower and wider valley bottoms. This may in part reflect the background of both groups, the Angles (and Danes) coming from an essentially lowland area with extensive arable cultivation, while other Norse peoples had a more pastoral, upland homeland. The pattern in Swaledale closely corresponds to this. Grinton was a Domesday vill, its name indicative of the middle phase of Anglian settlement from AD 750-950. None of the present settlements further up the valley with Norse names, for example Thwaite, Gunnerside and Keld, is mentioned in Domesday. This may be a reflection of the dispersed settlement pattern of discrete farmsteads still recognisable in some dales, such as Bishopdale and Dentdale, which preceded the development of nucleated villages.

Throughout the more marginal areas of the Dales control of grazing land would have been of prime importance - cattle, sheep, horses and pigs all contribute to placename formation on the margins of land suitable for cultivation. Graziers were increasingly interested in exercising exclusive rights to grazing - hence the common personal names attached to *erg* and *saetr*. Gunnerside is one of the Dales placenames which contains the element *saetr*, meaning a shieling, as well as a personal name, the Old Norse *Gunnarr*. The *saetr* names have been used to suggest that the Scandinavians introduced a summer pasture based economy into the Pennines, but it is equally likely that the seasonal movement of animals was an indigenous custom and that the Scandinavians merely carried on this tradition, or perhaps adapted some of the shieling sites for permanent settlement.

Settlements

One Viking period farmstead has been excavated in the Yorkshire Dales. Set on what is now almost bare limestone pavement, at 340m (1115ft) OD,

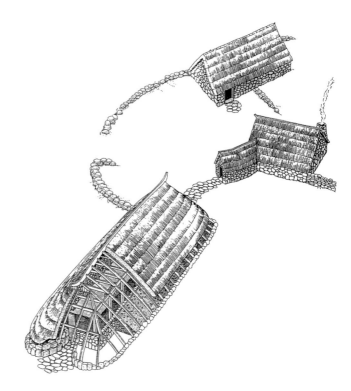

33 A suggested reconstruction of the Ribblehead farmstead, showing both straight gable ends and, as an alternative, hipped ends on the building in the foreground which was interpreted as a house. A flagged path leads from this building to a kitchen while the third building was probably a workshop. The earth and rubble infill between the outer edges of the walls of the house prevented rain being driven through the walls and provided some insulation. The roofs would have been covered with heather thatch or turves, possibly weighted down with stones, which would have allowed some smoke to escape.

close to the former Ribblehead quarry, are the remains of three rectangular buildings arranged around a small enclosure (**33**). To the north-east of this farmyard are two slightly larger plots enclosed by fragmentary limestone walls with to the south, on a glacial drift covered surface between two limestone terraces, two further fields covering about half a hectare.

The walls of the buildings were of dry rubble limestone, with rounded corners. The long walls of the house were 1.5 to 1.8m (5-6ft) thick while the south gable was of more massive construction with walls in places more than 3m (10ft) thick, the less solid north gable being 2.4m (8ft) thick. The outer-wall faces were formed from limestone boulders, the inner ones with coursed limestone slabs with rubble and earth providing a filling and insulation. All of the buildings would have had ridged roofs with a thatch or perhaps turf roof extending low down the outer edge of the walls to provide insulation and minimise the risk of water seeping in through the limestone walls. It is unclear whether these walls were load bearing or whether the weight of the roof was taken by cruck timbers. Load-bearing gable walls would have had to be thicker than the side walls to provide some load-bearing capability.

The largest building was 19m (62ft) long and 4m (13ft) wide internally and had centrally placed paved doorways in its gable ends. To the north lay a smaller building, with a doorway in the western end of the southern wall, approached by a double-walled paved passage pointing towards the larger building. The sandstone paving continued into the interior of the building, which had a small oven or kiln in the north-eastern corner. A third building, less well built than the other two, lay to the north-east. A broken sandstone hearth lay in the centre of its floor, while finds of iron rich cinders or scale, two sharpening or hammer stones and a lathe-turned spindle whorl suggest it was a workshop, possibly a smithy.

The smallest building contained, in addition to the oven or kiln, a concentration of small animal bones and a quern, leading to its interpretation as a kitchen. The majority of the animal bones were from cattle, sheep or goat and horse. Red deer and pig, possibly wild boar, were present in smaller quantities, together with some gamebirds and hare. No hearth was found in the main building, nor was there any evidence of housing for stock, although other finds included a small iron cow bell, a horse bit, a spearhead, two iron knives and four Northumbrian *stycas*. These

coins, found in or close to the west gable end of the main building, date to the third quarter of the ninth century. Most of the remains indicate a small, largely self- sufficient farmstead, but the coins and the position close to a former Roman road across the Pennines suggest links with a market economy.

No other definitely Norse sites have been excavated in the Yorkshire Dales, but the settlement sites at Simy Folds in Upper Teesdale display some of the features found at Ribblehead. Here three farmsteads are associated with field systems covering some 12ha (30 acres). Each consists of a long narrow building aligned east-west, with a smaller one at a right angle to it forming two sides of an enclosed yard. Two of the Simy Folds sites have a third building nearby. Two radiocarbon dates from charcoal found here indicate occupation in the eighth century.

Field survey and aerial photography have identified other sites with similarities to the Simy Folds and Ribblehead farmsteads. These include complexes at Braida Garth in Kingsdale, buildings on Greenber Edge in Wensleydale and parts of the Lea Green complex above Grassington. On the moorland grazing above Gunnerside the earthworks of an isolated rectangular building and small circular enclosure have been suggested as the original *saetr* of Gunnar. One problem with these buildings is the difficulty of differentiating them from shielings and possibly earlier structures. Extensive work on shielings in Cumbria and Northumberland suggests the main difference between shielings and farmsteads is whether or not the buildings are associated with enclosures. Dating, even of excavated examples, is difficult as there are few datable artifacts, but building features such as thick uncoursed walls with rounded corners, entrances at the gable ends and the use of boulder foundations may indicate Norse farmsteads. Function, however, is not always easy to determine as buildings may undergo changes in use and status: a farmstead may become a shieling and vice-versa. Such changes leave few

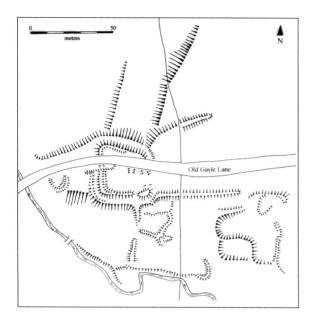

34 Old Gayle Lane, Hawes. The main subrectangular enclosure was surrounded by a bank and ditch and set within a series of low linear banks, the remains of a somewhat mutilated field system.

traces for the archaeologist to interpret. The picture becomes more confusing because shielings were often built in groups, forming temporary summer shelters for a number of households while many early medieval farmsteads were probably later reused as shielings. At Simy Folds one building at least appeared to have been rebuilt. Charcoal from a hearth in this building gave a radio-carbon date which suggested later reuse, perhaps associated with nearby finds of iron slag dated to the twelfth century. A hearth of probable Iron Age date underneath another building at Simy Folds suggests earlier use of a good settlement site.

Similar dating difficulties arise at the settlement complex on Lea Green, first excavated in 1893, where there are a group of circular and rectangular buildings, mainly within a subrectangular enclosure (**see 27**). The datable finds recognised during this excavation indicate occupation from the late Iron Age until the third century AD. The rectangular buildings, however,

similar in character to those of Ribblehead and Simy Folds, suggest the site was also occupied in the early medieval period. Similar buildings survive at Southerscales in Chapel le Dale although it is possible that these postdate the Norman Conquest (**colour plate 10**).

A two-roomed limestone building above Malham Tarn, excavated in the 1950's, was claimed as a possible Anglian hermitage on the basis of the discovery of part of a bronze brooch with a pierced Celtic interlace pattern and other bronze fragments interpreted as book fittings. A more domestic interpretation is possible.

The only other excavated site of comparable date in the Dales is the small rectangular earthwork bisected by Old Gayle Lane, Hawes (**34**). Prior to excavation, because of a similar morphology to some Roman signal stations and guardposts, this was thought to be a Roman military site. Excavation of the enclosure revealed a coursed drystone revetment or retaining wall around the summit of the bank. Within the enclosure were the footings of a barn or other agricultural building of medieval date. Immediately below this were slight remains of collapsed rough stone rubble of a small, probably partly timber-built, oval-shaped building or shelter. There were no finds of any kind relating to this phase. However organic material from primary silt in the ditch produced a radiocarbon date of 850 +/- 70 AD. The absence of finds and limited structural evidence make it difficult to interpret the site, which in appearance is similar to many supposed Iron Age enclosures found in lower ground to the east and north of the Dales.

The lack of pottery from excavated sites in the Dales suggests that the area may have become aceramic, relying on perishable wooden or wicker containers and recyclable metal instead. Beneath many of today's hamlets and farmsteads may be the traces of early medieval farmsteads, but continuity of occupied settlement sites is very difficult to prove.

5

CASTLES AND CROFTS: MONASTERIES AND MARKETS

The Norman Conquest resulted in a dramatic change in the landownership of the Yorkshire Dales. Although some members of the Northumbrian nobility submitted to William after his victory at Hastings in 1066, opposition to his rule continued. An uprising in 1068 was easily put down, but the following year there was more serious resistance, aided by a Danish invasion force. By Christmas 1069, however, William had secured his position and began the infamous 'Harrying of the North'. This was a deliberate attempt to make the north incapable of mounting an effective threat to the south of the country. The results are clearly indicated in the descriptions of the Domesday Book, compiled in 1086 to assist the administration of the new king throughout the country. This, the first public record, lists the new landowners and their estates, together with details of the pre-Conquest ownership. Most estates were worth considerably less than they had been in 1066 and many were described as 'waste'.

William's patronage had three main aims: to reward his supporters; to strengthen Norman control and colonisation of the country; to protect the boundaries of his newly won kingdom. Wensleydale and Swaledale, along with Teesdale and most of what is now still known as Richmondshire, were granted to Count Alan of Brittany and formed part of the new Honour of Richmond, one of the largest feudal holdings in the Country.

In Craven, Roger de Poitou was the dominant overlord. The division of lands resulted in a new political map, but except for the devastation caused by the Harrying of the North, the Conquest did not have an immediate effect on the native population who essentially found one overlord replaced by another. Some English landowners survived as tenants of Norman lords: Gospatric, for example, continued to hold the vills of Downholme and Thoresby and also became the tenant at Marrick and Askrigg.

Castles

The Norman landowners built castles to provide themselves with secure bases, to indicate their status and to act as centres for secular jurisdiction and administration. During the early years of the Conquest a string of motte and bailey castles was built on the western side of the Pennines to assist in the subjugation of the area. Castlehaw, the motte and bailey at Sedbergh, was strategically located on a prominent natural outcrop overlooking crossing points of the River Rawthey (**35**). Its steep-sided motte, an earthen mound some 11m (36ft) high, is surrounded on three sides by a wide ditch and by a natural scarp on the south. On the west a small bailey forms a raised terrace.

Most early castles were initially built of wood but unusually Richmond Castle, probably begun by Count Alan in 1071, used stone from the outset. It was carefully sited on a cliff above the River Swale, surrounded by a high stone wall with projecting towers adding to the strength of

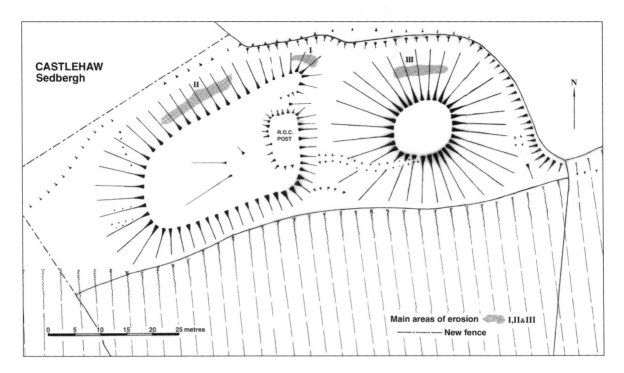

the defences. The two-storeyed Scollands Hall, Count Alan's main residence, dominated the interior. Timber-and-daub buildings inside the walls included lodgings for his household and garrison, stables, kitchens, bakehouse, brewhouse, laundry, smithy, carpenters shops and storehouses and barns.

A century later a rectangular keep, the Great Tower, was added. The walls and mural towers were strengthened and a barbican with moat and drawbridge constructed in front of the Great Tower. Unusually, this keep was built as an integrated part of the defences controlling the entrance to the castle and not just as a stronghold forming a last line of defence. It dominated the new town developing at the castle gates (**colour plate 11**). The town was not mentioned in the Domesday Survey of 1086 but by the beginning of the 14th century it had a population of nearly 600 in addition to the castle household. In the fourteenth century new chambers and a chapel were added to the north end of Scollands Hall. Richmond Castle was never tested by a prolonged siege and by the

35 Castlehaw, a motte-and-bailey castle near Sedbergh. Very little is known of its history, but in the twentieth century, during the Cold War, Castlehaw regained a military use when a Royal Observer Corps post was built in the bailey, partly below ground. The entrance to this post has now been sealed by concrete slabs.

sixteenth century it had fallen into disrepair.

Ribald, Count Alan's brother, built a motte and bailey castle on a ridge southwest of the present Middleham Castle. Williams Hill is a large earthen mound, about 12m (39ft) high, surrounded by a 6m (20ft) wide ditch, with a ditched, kidney-shaped bailey. The earthworks, abandoned in the second half of the twelfth century, are now partly covered by trees and scrub. The stone castle which replaced Williams Hill is dominated by a massive stone keep (**36**). The keep combined security with living quarters of considerable grandeur. The inner courtyard, originally surrounded by a timber palisade, and an outer courtyard to the east, now almost completely built over, housed further buildings

36 Williams Hill (foreground) and Middleham Castle. The two triangular market places indicate that Middleham was once the main market town in Wensleydale.

needed to support the Lord and his household, servants and retainers.

The Middleham estate was given to Richard, Duke of Gloucester, later Richard III, in 1471 and the castle became his preferred residence. It was seized by Henry VII after Richard was defeated in 1485 and thereafter the castle gradually fell into decay. It was garrisoned during the Civil War but, although used to house prisoners, it was not tested in battle.

Skipton and Bolton Castles were both involved in the Civil War. Bolton Castle was besieged by Parliamentary forces for over a year. The castle surrendered in November 1645 and was slighted two years later. Bolton had been built by Sir Richard Scrope, then Chancellor of England. It is said to have taken 18 years to build at a cost of 1000 marks per year, a total of £12,000, an immense sum for the time. A contract, signed in 1378 with master mason John Lewyn, included details of the heights of the curtain wall and towers, wall thicknesses, and

the functions of the rooms required. Much of the sandstone for the castle was quarried from Ellerlands Edge, a few hundred metres to the west. Here Stephen Moorhouse has identified an extensive series of quarries and traces of associated buildings and smithies. According to Leland, the Tudor antiquarian, the oak roof timbers were cut in Engleby in Cumberland and hauled by oxen to Bolton, presumably because there were no suitable trees in the Wensleydale area.

The Castle has recently benefited from a major consolidation programme (**see 47**). Its massive corner towers and position, carefully sited to dominate much of Wensleydale and Bishopdale, give a great impression of strength but this is somewhat of an illusion. There is no moat or ditch to prevent the use of siege towers and no drawbridge. Bolton was not intended as a military citadel. Instead, domestic and military functions were integrated into a single building which provided considerable variation in the scale and status of the accommodation in the various apartments. The ground floor provided stables and stores while the principal rooms were on the first floor, approached from the central courtyard. The Great Hall was on the north range, with the private apartments to the west and domestic offices to the east. There were twelve independent lodgings of one or two rooms for retainers.

Several windows were enlarged in the sixteenth-century to provide more light to the apartments within. In 1568 Bolton Castle was chosen by Queen Elizabeth for the custody of Mary Queen of Scots. By then it was surrounded by extensive landscaped grounds, including a sunken garden, and a series of walled deer parks within which the earthworks of two hunting towers have been identified.

Hunting

Hunting was a favourite pastime of Norman lords. Large areas of the upper Dales are described in medieval documents as 'forest' or 'free chase'. This does not necessarily mean these areas were densely wooded, although they contained considerably more woodland than in later centuries, or that they were uninhabited, but refers to their distinctive legal status designed to preserve game. A forest needed both open country for the hunt and woodland to shelter and feed the main game animals: fallow, red and roe deer and wild boar. Forest status also placed the area directly under the control of a feudal landowner.

Placenames such as New Forest, Langstrothdale Chase, and the Forest of Barden provide clues to the locations of some of the hunting areas. Bainbridge village was developed in the twelfth century to manage the Forest of Wensleydale, sometimes known as the Forest of Bainbridge. In 1229 Ranulph, Lord of Middleham, stated that the town of 'Beyntbridge belonged to his ancestors by service of keeping the forest, so that they might have abiding there twelve foresters, and that every forester should have there one dwelling house and nine acres of land'.

Hunting was also practised by church leaders: in 1179 the monks of Bridlington Priory complained that when the Archdeacon of Richmond visited their church at Grinton his retinue included ninety-seven horses, twenty-one

dogs and three hawks. Many early grants of land to the monasteries excluded hunting rights. The first gifts from the Mowbray family to Fountains and Byland Abbeys, for example, protected the Mowbrays' hunting interests. The monks of Byland were allowed to take from Backstone Beck whatever they needed for their lodges and cattle-folds and were allowed to cut hay but not to cultivate any arable land except for herb patches. They might keep little dogs but fierce dogs had to be chained up. They could keep thirty sows and their young of up to two years of age and five boars but these had to be removed from the area between 8 June and 10 July each year 'on account of the young of the deer'. Any lay shepherds employed by the abbey had to take an oath that they would not poach game. In 1172 money problems forced Roger de Mowbray to make further 'grants' to Byland Abbey. These included a right to clear land for arable cultivation but de Mowbray retained the hunting rights.

The feudal landowners developed various strategies to exploit their forests. These included encouraging settlement by tenants or selling summer grazing rights on the fells as well as granting land to monastic houses. A patchwork of monastic, demesne and peasant settlements existed in most forest areas by the fourteenth century and can still be traced in the present settlement pattern. Economic growth, however, also enabled the larger landowners to create enclosed deer parks specifically for hunting. These parks, surrounded by banks, ditches and stone walls, were not static landscape features but were enlarged or made smaller according to economies and fashion. Some gradually changed into amenity parks but still provided visible status and a supply of fresh food throughout the year, often from rabbit warrens or fishponds. Purpose-built warrens, like that at Ellerlands by Castle Bolton, had artificial pillow mounds for the rabbits to burrow into (**37**). The Neville estate contained six deer parks, mainly close to Middleham although Scale Park, created in 1410, lay on the borders of the estate at Kettlewell (**see 32**).

37 The raised mounds and rectangular enclosure of the artificial rabbit warren at Ellerlands, Castle Bolton overlie the remains of a co-axial field system. The quarries at the top of the photograph, now covered by scrub, supplied stone for the castle.

Henry Clifford rebuilt Barden Tower in Wharfedale, originally one of six lodges in the Forest of Barden, after regaining his family estates in 1485, and surrounded it with the Little Park and the much larger Rough Park. A rabbit warren was established east of the river. The Little Park also included a fishpond complex, now reutilised for trout breeding. A separate chapel to the south of the Tower was built in 1516/17 (**38**). Barden Tower was neglected after his death, and plundered during the Civil War but an inscription on the south wall of the Tower records its subsequent restoration and enlargement by his great great granddaughter, the redoubtable Lady Anne Clifford, in 1658. She had been born in Skipton Castle in 1590. Twice widowed, she succeeded, after the Civil War and a long struggle, to the vast Clifford estate which extended almost continuously from Skipton to Brougham near Penrith. In her later years she traveled by horse litter, with an extensive retinue, overseeing work on the estate and left a diary of her journeys and work.

The Norton family, neighbours and rivals of the Cliffords, built an observation tower on the edge of their estate at Rylstone. Only the outer walls survive, occupying a prominent position on the flanks of Barden Moor. Norton Tower, partly surrounded by a broad bank, ditch and wall, overlooks a series of pillow mounds and other cairns and may have been used to keep watch for poachers from the Clifford's estate. The Rylstone estates were confiscated by the Crown after Richard Norton took part in the Rising of the North in 1569. Although the site of their late-fifteenth-century house is now occupied by modern farmbuildings, much of its extensive formal sunken gardens survive.

The monasteries

In the century after the Norman Conquest large areas of the Dales came under monastic control. The monastic estates developed piecemeal, initially through endowments from the great Norman lords in return for prayers for the souls of themselves and their families, but were subsequently consolidated by purchase and exchange. Before the Dissolution of the Monasteries by Henry VIII between 1536 and 1540 most of the Dales was in monastic hands.

Most of the monasteries were based outside or on the fringes of the Dales. In Swaledale the

38 Barden Tower was rebuilt by Henry Lord Clifford after he made Barden the centre of his Yorkshire estates in 1485. The Tower was still complete in 1774 but had become ruinous thirty years later. The heavily buttressed tower attached to the Chapel was for banqueting. Other buildings survive as earthworks.

major landowners included Rievaulx Abbey, Bridlington Priory and Easby Abbey. Coverham Abbey owned most of Coverdale. Furness and Sawley Abbeys had lands in the western Dales, Byland Abbey had lands in Nidderdale, Fountains Abbey had extensive estates in Airedale, Wharfedale and Nidderdale and Bolton Priory lands in Lower Wharfedale and Airedale. Jervaulx Abbey controlled much of Wensleydale, particularly the upper dale, where placenames such as High and Low Abbotside give clues to its landholdings. Initially called Fors Abbey, it had been founded in upper Wensleydale in the eleventh century and moved to its present site in 1156. During construction of the Wensleydale railway c.1877 burials were discovered close to Grange Gill Beck. Jervaulx Abbey had a grange

39 Bolton Priory, located on a narrow terrace beside the River Wharfe. The present road follows the line of the precinct wall. The aqueduct crossing the road serves a later mill but the canons had at least one mill and a tannery inside the monastic precinct. The lay workforce at Bolton, which probably numbered about 200 early in the fourteenth century lived outside the precinct. The Priory accounts for 1312/3 list 101 lay workers based here, including 48 oxherds and 23 other herdsmen. Smaller numbers were employed on the Priory's other estates.

here until the Dissolution. The grange would have included the former Fors Abbey site but the precise location of the monastic buildings has not been identified.

The Augustinian canons who founded Bolton Priory initially settled at Embsay in 1120. In 1135

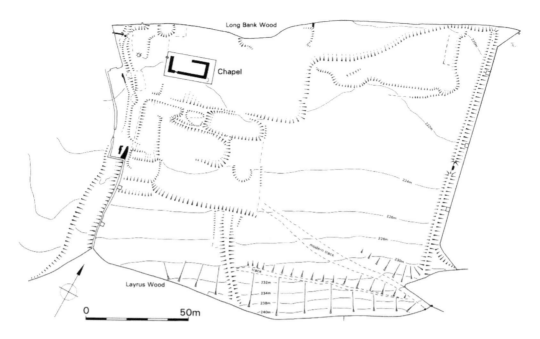

Long Bank Wood

Chapel

Layrus Wood

0   50m

40 Plan of the Knights Templar's Preceptory, West Witton. The ruined chapel and the earthworks of the Inner Court, above Temple Farm, mark the centre of a small estate which in 1307 had arable land and 589 animals, mainly sheep and pigs.

they were given the manor of Bolton and moved to the present site close to the River Wharfe (**39**). Construction of the church began c.1170 and continued throughout the priory's history. The West Tower, begun in 1520, had not been completed by the Dissolution and was not roofed until 1985. The nave became the parish church after the Dissolution, but the presbytery and north transept only survive to eaves height. Bolton Hall incorporates the fourteenth-century gatehouse to the priory and some of the precinct wall is still in use. The outlines of some other buildings, including the chapter house and cloisters, have been exposed by excavation. The ponds were tanks for the tannery which lay inside the monastic precinct. The large aisled barn here, probably the largest timber-framed building in Northern England, is now thought to be of post-medieval date.

Building work started at Coverham Abbey, a Premonstratensian house, sometime between 1196 and 1202, after the monks had transferred from their original site at Swainby in the Vale of Mowbray, possibly to be closer to their patrons based at Middleham Castle. The early-sixteenth-century abbots' quarters and guesthouse were converted into a private house after the Dissolution, the north range being rebuilt as a compact, but high-quality, house c.1800. Its garden contains the remains of the south arcade of the abbey church. The gatehouse also survives but the fishponds to the east were built over in the early 1980s. North of the parish church at Coverham are the earthworks of a medieval mill pond and farm complex.

One of the minor monastic orders, the Knights Templar, initially founded to protect pilgrims, had a preceptory at West Witton until the order was suppressed in 1307. The ruins of the chapel and the earthworks of the Inner Court survive above Temple Farm (**40**). An earlier manor complex lay to the north. The boundaries of this estate, which like most other monastic land was tithe free, can still be traced, sometimes as earthworks. A series of stones, each inscribed with a Maltese cross, mark places where through

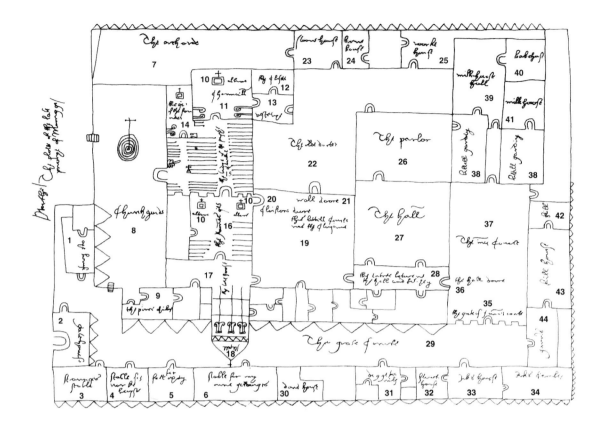

1 oxe howse	16 the Nonnes quier	30 dove howse
2 gatehowse	17 the bell house	31 dogge kennels
3 straungers stable	18 stepill	32 Slawter howse
4 stable for worke horsse	19 this littell Courte was the Cloisture	33 Joks howse
5 for fatt oxen	20 Cloistore doore	34 Joks chamber
6 stable for my owne geldings	21 wall doore	35 the gate of the inner courte
7 The orcharde	22 The olde dorter	36 the hall doore
8 Churchyarde	23 stoore howse	37 The inner Courte
9 the priores chamber	24 brewe howse	38 littell garden
10 altare	25 worke howse	39 milkhowse hall
11 Chancell	26 The parlor	40 bakehowse
12 the closett	27 The hall	41 milk howse
13 vestereye	28 the entree betwene the hall and kitchen	42 kiln
14 the quier of the founder	29 The grate Courte	43 kiln howse
15 the bodye of the paryshe churche		44 garners

41 A ground plan of the Marrick Priory site c.1585, nearly fifty years after the nuns had left. Most of the priory buildings were still substantially intact although many had different functions.

routes entered the estate, but the surviving examples are either recut or nineteenth-century replacements.

Most monastic institutions were for men, but within the Dales a Benedictine nunnery was founded close to the River Swale at Marrick c. 1154. A few years later a Cistercian nunnery was founded less than a mile away at Ellerton. Ellerton was always a small, poorly endowed house. Today all that is visible is a ruined church. This is surrounded by indistinct earthworks but geophysical survey has traced the details of the cloister and other buildings.

Marrick, which was the richest nunnery in Yorkshire, though still poor when compared with the male houses, had a prioress and sixteen nuns and a gross income of £64.18.9 when it was surrendered in 1539. After the Dissolution it became the centre of a small estate, although the Priory church continued to be used as a place of worship for the parish. A detailed survey and map of c. 1585 suggests that most of the priory buildings were then still standing (41). Now only the church, part of the prioress's house, short lengths of the precinct wall and a farmhouse which incorporates part the refectory, survive above ground, although earthworks indicate the remains of other buildings to the east of the church. The area around the priory contains fishponds and traces of earlier tofts and crofts.

Fountains Abbey played a very important part in the development of the medieval landscape, even though it lay outside the Dales. Fountains, founded in 1132, became the richest Cistercian house in England and one of the most powerful monasteries in the north. Through a series of grants, exchanges and purchases it amassed a considerable estate, particularly in Lower Wensleydale, Nidderdale, Upper Wharfedale, Littondale and Airedale, recorded by placenames such as Fountains Fell. The estate was organised into granges, initially managed directly by the abbey. Most had a mixed farming base but specialised to concentrate on different stages of animal husbandry or to exploit specific resources. Iron and lead were mined and

smelted in Nidderdale, Malham Tarn was used as a fishery. Sheep farming, however, was the most important. The limestone pastures and fells of Craven served as extensive sheep runs, controlled from granges and smaller lodges, many of which later developed into hamlets or isolated farms. By the end of the thirteenth century Fountains had a flock of about 15,000 sheep. The Abbey traded directly with Italian merchants and receipts from the sale of wool alone amounted to almost three times its income from other sources. A system of transhumance was developed whereby some flocks spent the summer months on the Craven moorlands but overwintered on lower granges in Nidderdale and near the abbey.

The buildings of the lodges, sheephouses and granges were extensive features in their own right but the accompanying grazing grounds could cover hundreds of hectares. Granges were often sited near the head of small valleys so as to utilise the rough grazing on the moor tops and pastures on the valley sides. The Bolton Priory bercary or sheep farm at Malham gives an idea of the scale of grange buildings (42). The bercary is set into a shallow valley, taking advantage of the limestone scars on either side. The main area is enclosed by boulder walls and the interior subdivided into a number of different sized enclosures. A rectangular sheephouse measuring some 14.5 by 5.5m (48 by 18ft) internally, lay on the north boundary while other buildings lay against the western side. These buildings did not function in isolation as the grazing grounds also contained isolated shepherds' huts and sheep folds, often with run-in walls to assist flock management.

Kilnsey formed the administrative centre for Fountains Abbey's estates in Upper Craven. An extensive complex of buildings and enclosures on Outgang Hill formed the central point for shearing and washing the flocks from the grazing grounds of Fountains Fell (43). The gatehouse at Kilnsey Old Hall may be the remnants of the court house of the grange. More than a hundred grange sites are known from documents, many of which can be identified as hamlets or farms today. At the Dissolution the vast estates owned by the monastic houses passed to the Crown. They were then sold, often to London-based speculators or to local lords. Much of Littondale, for example, was acquired by the Cliffords of Skipton, and the Bolton Priory estates by the Earl of Cumberland. Less powerful local families, many of whom had held lay positions under the monasteries or had leased granges and other land, acquired smaller estates. Some families bought from speculators, others had pre-Dissolution deals with the monasteries.

A network of roads and trackways linked the monastic estates with their mother houses. The best-known of these is Mastiles Lane, which provided a route between Fountains Abbey and its estates in Kilnsey, Malham and the Lake District. The bases of some of the wayside crosses which marked the route still survive on Malham Moor. Medieval routes can sometimes be identified through the mapping of references to roads and bridges in contemporary documents.

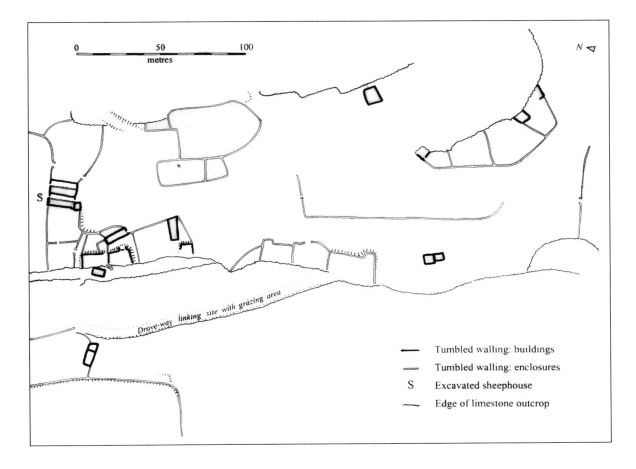

Drove-way linking site with grazing area

——— Tumbled walling: buildings

— Tumbled walling: enclosures

S   Excavated sheephouse

‿‿ Edge of limestone outcrop

42 A plan of the buildings and enclosures at the centre of the Bolton Priory bercary at Malham. The main sheephouse was excavated by Arthur Raistrick in 1952-3. The enclosures and structures take advantage of the limestone outcrops. After Moorhouse and Raistrick.

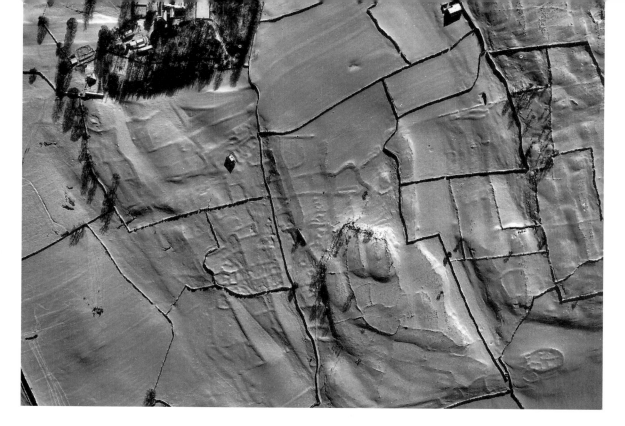

43 Outgang Hill, Kilnsey. A light snow cover highlights the grassy banks of a complex group of small enclosures overlain by post-medieval field walls. The enclosures formed part of the Fountains Abbey grange at Kilnsey.

Several roads in Upper Nidderdale, where the easiest routes to the Byland estates were across Fountains' land, were the subject of agreements between the two abbeys. Byland gained a right to use two roads and to build a bridge at Ramsgill but elsewhere their animals were not to pasture on Fountains' land except when they were held up by floods.

Although most tracks were only used by packhorses and to drive stock, others were suitable for long-distance travel by the king and his retinue, and for transporting bulky or heavy materials. Many routes were on the valley sides. A few are still used as roads, others have been downgraded to bridleways and footpaths or abandoned altogether as a result of changes in the settlement pattern or of improved land

drainage which has enabled travelling along the valley floor.

Few medieval bridges have survived the floods of succeeding centuries, but the ribbed arches of some stone bridges can still be appreciated, especially from below. They include the small single-arched Bow Bridge at Low Abbotside, widened for the Richmond and Lancaster Turnpike in the eighteenth century and replaced in 1899 by a new bridge; the downstream half of Marske bridge; and the downstream part of the bridge across the Ure at Wensley (44).

Wapentake, parish, church and township

In the medieval period, secular administration, as today, functioned at a complex variety of levels. The Dales occupy the western parts of the former North and West Ridings of Yorkshire. The term 'Riding', a third part, is Scandinavian in origin. This suggests that these large units were organised after Halfdan conquered Northumbria in 876. The ridings were subdivided into 'wapentakes', groupings of townships. Some townships were further subdivided into hamlets. Townships and hamlets were the communities of peasant farmers whose activities supported the Anglo-Scandinavian aristocracy and, after 1066, the Norman lords and their followers. Much medieval activity relied on co-operation between members of a community, whether for organising crop rotations, sharing oxen to build up a full plough team, the control of common pasture rights, or sharing access to other resources: timber for building, underwood for fuel and hedging, peat and turves for fuel or bracken, heather and rushes for bedding and roofing materials. Community co-operation was generally organised at the hamlet or township level, later formalised by the system of manorial courts. Townships continued into the nineteenth century, many boundaries being marked on the 6" Ordnance Survey maps of the 1850s, often defined by physical banks and ditches, natural features such as watercourses or by intermittent markers such as cairns or crosses, normally positioned in prominent locations (**45**).

Parishes, which often consisted of several townships, were initially of mainly ecclesiastical significance. They were probably later in date than the townships but grew in importance with the economic power of the church. Some ecclesiastical parishes were huge. Grinton parish, for example, encompassed all of Upper Swaledale, while Aysgarth covered most of Wensleydale, Bishopdale and their side valleys. Because of their vast size, chapels of ease were built to make it easier for parishioners to attend church services. Some, like those at Hawes, Hudswell, Muker and Dent, later developed into parish churches in their own right while others, like the now ruined example at Stalling Busk, continued as chapels. St Simon's Chapel in Coverdale, also now a ruin, suffered the indignity of being used as an alehouse in 1586.

Settlements

The period between the Harrying of the North

44 Wensley Bridge. The pointed arches of the downstream half of the bridge were probably built in the fifteenth century with £40 left by Richard, the first Lord Scrope, for the repair of an earlier bridge. The later arches on the upstream half of the bridge have a more rounded profile.

and the early fourteenth century was one of rising population and economic expansion. The monasteries were as keen as other landowners to maximise the returns from their estates. Title deeds show that Bridlington Priory and Rievaulx Abbey extended pastoral farming in Upper Swaledale in the twelfth and thirteenth centuries with a series of assarts and enclosed meadows establishing extensive vaccaries and bercaries. Numerous placenames record a gradual assarting or reclamation of land from the waste. Prior to the Conquest much of the settlement pattern seems to have been based on dispersed farmsteads and as pressure on land grew, many shielings, temporary dwellings on land used as summer pasture, were converted into permanent farms. This process is hinted at by placenames such as Appersett and Marsett.

Much of the present-day settlement pattern has its origins in the medieval period. Many villages and hamlets owe their origins to granges established by the monasteries. Others lie astride important routeways and thus appear to be street villages, although closer examination

45 County, wapentake, ecclesiastical parish and township boundaries in the Yorkshire Dales National Park. Many of the townships, especially the larger ones, were also subdivided into hamlets. By the time they were mapped by the Ordnance Survey in the mid-nineteenth century some township divisions had been amalgamated. Areas of moorland were sometimes common to more than one township. KM - Kirkby Malham, CC - Cold Cotes (detached), Cg - Cogden, Cr - Crackpot, EG - East Grinton, Hk - Harkerside, SL - Summer Lodge, SP - Scale Park, WG - West Grinton.

frequently reveals evidence for organised planning with rows of well-defined toft boundaries. A toft is essentially a single tenurial unit: a house, outbuildings, garden, yards and small enclosures belonging to one person. Regular village greens and back lanes behind toft boundaries also indicate planned settlements, some possibly laid out on new sites after the Harrying of the North or in the twelfth century, although others may have evolved as early as the ninth century. There are hints of Scandinavian origins for some planned Dales

1 An artist's impression of the landscape by Victoria Cave 11,000 years ago. A herd of reindeer browse warily while in the valley bottom hunters butcher their kill.

2 Malham Tarn, naturally dammed by a glacial moraine, provided a wide range of food resources for Mesolithic hunter-gatherers. Thousands of pieces of flint have been found between the lake and the higher ground to the north.

3 Cup and ring marks on a sandstone slab on Gayles Moor.

4 Earthworks of a late prehistoric co-axial field system above Grassington. The area reverted to common grazing land until it was enclosed in 1792. The unusual pattern of the enclosure walls shows the importance placed on ensuring that stock had access to a small stream for water.

5 Maiden Castle. Despite the large size of the ditch surrounding this hillside enclosure, rising land and dead ground to the south means that it was very badly sited for defensive purposes. The stone avenue may be a later addition but its function remains obscure.

6 The sharp outline and greener colour of grass growing on silted up ditches revealed the playing card shape of a Roman Fort near the River Ure at Wensley during the dry summer of 1995. Other green marks show the position of silt in former river channels.

7 Excavation in progress on a late prehistoric settlement at Healaugh, Swaledale, showing the stone flagged floor of a circular building. The building is partly scooped into the hillside and extends, on the downslope side, on to a small terrace.

8 The top of the lynchets and stone banked enclosures at Thornsber barn are picked out by parching. Part of the circular enclosure in the foreground was excavated in 1968.

9 The Gargrave villa as it may have appeared in the later third century. J Dobie after M Stroud.

10 The stone bases of long, early medieval buildings at Southerscales, Chapel le Dale

11 Richmond Castle and market place. Richmond town is not mentioned in the Domesday Survey of 1086 but by the beginning of the 14th century it had a population of nearly 600 in addition to the castle household. Planned burgage plots radiate from the market place towards the line of the town walls. The walls enclosed an area of over 7 ha (18 acres), nearly half of which consisted of the castle and its defences.

12 Grinton was the centre of one of the largest medieval parishes in the country, possibly supplanting an earlier territorial unit. In 1540 John Leland described Grinton as a little market town with a market of corn and linen cloth. Its houses were partly slated, partly thatched. It has declined in economic importance and earthworks show that it has also declined in size.

13 East Witton town as portrayed in a map of 1627 by William Senior, "Professor of Arithmetique, Geometrie, Astronomie, Navigation and Dialling".

14 The patchwork of hay meadows and field barns at Gunnerside Bottoms, an infilled glacial lake.

15 The bouse teams at the Sir Francis Mine in Gunnerside Gill. Ore-rich rock was stored here and sorted by hand before being sent to the crushing mill in the background.

16 Grinton is the best-preserved lead smelt mill in the Yorkshire Dales. The massive timber supports for the bellows still survive although most of the stonework of the two ore hearths and the slag hearth has disappeared.

villages as surveys of some common fields have evidence of 'solskifte', a regular distribution of lands within the fields according to the position of a toft within the village. In some planned villages, greens are particularly evident: nearly square, as at Bainbridge, Redmire and Reeth or rectangular, as at Arncliffe and West Burton (**46**). Houses set back from the road edge can indicate the position of a former green as at Cracoe. Not all rows of tofts in a settlement are contemporary: villages have expanded, contracted and sometimes disappeared altogether. Nearly all villages in the Dales, however, are agricultural in origin, with tofts the home bases of farming communities who supported themselves by growing grain and raising stock. Greenhow Hill, a straggling group of cottages and smallholdings between Pateley Bridge and Grassington, is the only settlement thought to have been deliberately founded to house miners, although many villages and hamlets did expand to house miners and other industrial workers.

Greens do not necessarily indicate early planning. Sir Richard Scrope is unlikely to have wanted peasants as close to his imposing castle as the position of the present village of Castle Bolton would imply, although the adjacent church, physically dominated by the castle, may have been acceptable for convenience and as a symbol of the relative importance of secular and ecclesiastical power (**47**). The village's regular plan indicates that it was deliberately laid out. However, the plan may not be a survival from a pre-castle planned settlement. Instead, it may postdate the slighting of the castle after the Civil War and the Powlet family's construction, in 1678, of a new mansion, Bolton Hall, in parkland close to the River Ure, some 4.5km (3 miles) to the south-east. A series of building platforms at the east end of the village possibly represents an

46 The rectangular green and the regularity of the hedgerows and stone walls which mark many of the toft boundaries suggest that at least part of West Burton is a medieval planned village.

47 The quadrangular form of Bolton Castle dominates St Oswald's Church and the village of Castle Bolton. The deep hollow on the west of the castle is a sunken garden and not part of a moat. In the eighteenth and early nineteenth centuries the castle was used as cottages and there was a farmhouse in the small rectangular fields to the south.

earlier focus. Further east still are the remains of a watermill and farmstead, partly in a field called Grange Garth, which have been identified as the vicarage which moved from north of the castle to the east end of the village in 1403. This complex may have been shortlived as the area was meadowland a little over a century later.

Grinton, described as a market town for corn and linen in 1540, is a good example of how settlements change. The bridge and St Andrew's church, together with Blackburn Hall which was initially built by the canons of Bridlington Priory, form the focus of the village. The main route from the bridge was originally south towards Leyburn: the older houses, many of which date from the mid-seventeenth century, all front this street, and there are also traces of regular toft and croft earthworks on its east side and more irregular earthworks on the west side. In 1836, the Reeth-Richmond turnpike cut a new route through fields at the northern edge of the village and most development since has been alongside this new road. An earlier track, still a footpath, is recognisable as a holloway (**colour plate 12**).

Late-medieval accounts for Bishopdale township, examined by Stephen Moorhouse, list thirty separate tenements. Some are still recognisable as farms but twenty-two are now only identifiable as earthworks or field names. Bishopdale also includes two settlements, Eshington and Crooksby, which were recorded in the Domesday Book of 1086 but which appear to have been abandoned by the late thirteenth century. Their location can also be identified through placenames. The three main villages in Bishopdale today, West Burton, Newbiggin and Thoralby, all contain the earthworks of former building plots and are bypassed by the present road along the valley floor: earlier routes linking them with the dispersed farmsteads survive in part as earthworks and footpaths.

The reasons why some villages flourished while others declined or even disappeared altogether are normally complex but often owe more to the influence of manorial lords and their policies of estate management than to climatic deterioration, the impact of diseases such as the Black Death or sacking by Scottish raiders and general economic fluctuations. Walburn (**48**) is perhaps the most impressive deserted village in the Dales. It is not known when the village earthworks were abandoned, but enclosure of its common fields had begun in the fifteenth century while successive lords of the manor converted freehold land into leasehold land in order to increase their rents. The earthworks of West Bolton are more complex. Field survey has identified the remains of regular toft and croft earthworks, partly overlain by a later medieval sheephouse and trackways and two post-medieval farms set within self-contained enclosures. The earthworks are surrounded by a complex pattern of cultivation ridges, parts of which were still developing after the village had been abandoned.

At first glance East Witton appears to be an early nineteenth-century estate village, contemporary with the church of 1809 which was built by the Earl of Ailesbury in honour of George III's jubilee. A map of 1627 shows a very similar layout although the then parish church lay to the south-east of the village (**colour plate 13; 49**) Seventeen houses lay along a straggling lane between it and the village green. At the Dissolution, East Witton, owned by Jervaulx Abbey, had fifty-three households. In 1377 it had had 220 taxpayers. It is likely that the monks, who had gained control of the township by the late thirteenth century, planned the development of the new village site around a suitable market place for a market and cattle fair first held in 1307. Despite their support East Witton faced stiff competition from the market at nearby Middleham, granted a charter in 1389, and failed to prosper as a town.

48 The deserted medieval village of Walburn. Despite proximity to the Leyburn-Richmond road and the sixteenth-century fortified manor house of Walburn Hall, these impressive village earthworks were not recognised until 1992. They lie within an extensive area of well-preserved ridge and furrow, fossilised under later enclosure walls, but the remains of the crofts and tofts clearly show the plan of the village which is bisected by a small stream.

49 East Witton. The walled closes behind most of the houses are clearly identifiable as the toft boundaries shown on the 1627 map (reproduced as colour plate 13). The main road system has changed and there are now no buildings on the green.

The more successful market towns, Richmond, Sedbergh, Settle and Skipton all lay on the fringes of the Dales, closer to better agricultural land. Leyburn was a latecomer, granted a market charter by Charles II, but it displaced both Middleham and Wensley which had been granted a charter in 1202. In the late thirteenth and early fourteenth centuries some more central settlements, including Grassington, Carperby and Appletreewick, aspired to markets and fairs. Carperby's impressive market cross, set on a flight of steps and decorated with the initials RB, the date 1674 and two carved faces, still survives, but its market failed. It was succeeded by Askrigg, granted a market charter

in 1587, which in turn declined due to competition from Hawes. Hawes began to flourish when the Richmond to Lancaster turnpike was diverted through the town instead of over Cam Fell in 1795 and strengthened its position when the railway arrived in 1878. Throughout the twentieth century its market, particularly for sheep, was an important focus of agricultural and community life.

6

'THE SOILE ABOUT IS VERY HILLY AND BERITH LITLE CORNE BUT NORISETH MANY BESTES'

Agriculture was the main economic activity in the Dales for thousands of years, but for most of these the only indications we have are archaeological: pollen analysis, the pattern of field systems, tools such as querns and, very rarely, identification of crop and weed seeds found in buried soils during archeological excavation. The local population would have been agriculturally self-sufficient for most of this time and their exports of agricultural produce limited to the taxation of the Roman army and possibly of earlier tribal overlords. Not until the medieval period do we get any documentary evidence to supplement the archaeological record. Later travellers through the Dales often recorded their impressions of the landscape. The chapter heading, a description of Wensleydale by the Tudor antiquarian, John Leland, still bears true today.

The accounts and other documents produced by the monasteries give some details about overall food production and consumption and help to provide a fuller picture of medieval agricultural activity. Although most of the food consumed was still grown in the area, the monasteries imported fish, wine and other delicacies and their efficient marketing contacts enabled wool and other animal products to be exported.

Medieval field systems

Although arable cultivation today only occurs on the fringes of the Dales, there are extensive remains of arable fields of medieval and later date, particularly in Lower Wensleydale and Bishopdale, Wharfedale and Malhamdale. Lynchets and ridge and furrow - rolling, parallel strips divided by headlands - are the most characteristic surviving features of medieval arable fields. The strips, which give some fields a corrugated effect, enabled land of differing qualities to be fairly distributed amongst all tenants of a township. They are generally associated with nucleated settlements. These meant that each farmer was centrally placed to manage strips scattered throughout the fields. Each holding was ploughed individually. The single furrow plough, drawn by oxen or horses, went up one side and down the other side of a strip, and created the ridge by constantly turning the sod towards the centre. A slight curve, often a reverse S-shape, helped the plough team to turn round without encroaching on the next strip. The shapes and sizes of strips varied, generally according to the lie of the land and the type of soil (**see 19**).

Exactly why ridge and furrow was created is unclear: it was not necessary to create ridges when ploughing. Ridges defined individual strips, but perhaps equally significantly assisted in drainage, marginally increased the area of land under cultivation and provided some insurance against climatic variation. Crops in the furrows would grow better in dry summers than those on the better-drained ridges, the opposite being true in wet seasons.

50 Lynchets and ridge and furrow overlying earlier field systems and butting up to a Romano-British settlement at Gordale.

Cultivation ridges were subject to modification: strips could be subdivided, shortened or extended as pressure on land varied. Dating is therefore difficult. Some cultivation ridges are clearly earlier than overlying field walls but others were ploughed as late as the nineteenth century and even the early twentieth century at times of corn shortage caused by wars. Eighteenth- and nineteenth-century ploughing, however, generally produced straighter, narrower ridges.

Lynchets, which can be up to 300m (330yds) long, tend to dominate where arable farming has taken place on steeper slopes (**50**). Some are almost indistinguishable from ridge and furrow, but others form distinct broader terraces. These are generally between 9 and 20m (30-65ft) wide, parallel with the contours, with banks caused by both soil-creep down a slope and by deliberate revetment of stones disturbed by ploughing. The terraces provided a flatter surface for ploughing and sometimes still have traces of ridge and furrow on them. A few groups of lynchets run across the contours and must have been particularly prone to soil erosion when ploughed.

Although the common arable fields were subject to piecemeal enclosure, some arable land continued to be communally farmed in the seventeenth century. Thus the 1605 survey of the Lordship of Middleham records three common fields at West Witton and four at West Burton. Further up Wensleydale the 17 acre (7ha) Corn Close at Worton was shared between 12 tenants. The name and co-tenancies suggest that this may have been just the remnant of a former larger field. At Wensley, open-field agriculture survived until the end of the century although arable cultivation was then in decline as wool and meat production became more attractive.

The area under cultivation varied as pressure on land changed. Cultivation ridges can be found at altitudes of up to 350m (1150ft) and on land that is vulnerable to winter flooding, but in general their distribution reflects the extent of medieval arable agriculture. This reached a peak between AD 1100 and 1300 and began to decline in the fourteenth century, mainly as a result of climatic deterioration and the population collapse after the Black Death of 1348-9.

Crops and livestock

A range of arable crops was grown during the medieval period. The accounts of Bolton Priory, most of whose granges lay in the Dales, record oats, wheat, rye, barley and beans. Oats were the main cereal crop because of their ability to withstand the climate, but were less productive than other cereals. Crop yields varied considerably from year to year, being particularly low in the second decade of the fourteenth century. Sodden pastures and a lack of hay also affected livestock and encouraged disease. In 1320, Bolton Priory's flock fell by two thirds to 913 while its cattle herd, which had numbered 503 a few years earlier, crashed to 31. Cow's milk was converted to butter and cheese for storage. Ewes were also milked with some 25 per cent of

the Priory's cheese being made with sheep's milk.

Arable farming demanded animal husbandry, not only for the plough teams but to provide manure to fertilise the fields. Most manure came from animals and their bedding but domestic waste, night soil, ash, animal bones and carcasses and the remains of worn out roofing materials such as turf, ling and bracken were also used. The effect of manuring could be concentrated by keeping and feeding animals on lower ground during the winter. This system developed, once arable farming became less common, into the hay meadow-field barn cycle described below. Higher ground, unsuitable for arable farming, provided an extensive grazing resource particularly during the summer months. In some townships farmers had to bring their animals down from the grazing pastures overnight. This had the effect of increasing summer manuring on the enclosed land.

The number of animals it was possible to keep over the winter was determined not by the total amount of grazing available, but by the more restricted availability of winter feed. This feed included both sheltered winter grazing and the supplement offered by hay and, to a lesser extent, straw and even leaves, holly in particular being recorded as a winter foodstuff.

Community control

Open-field farming and the grazing of unenclosed land belonging to a township was strictly controlled by the community, but was subject to change. At the beginning of the fifteenth century the common fields of Walburn were divided into North, South and West Fields. These would be used, in a three-year rotation, for winter-sown crops of wheat and rye, spring-sown crops of barley, oats, peas and beans, or left as fallow. By the end of the century just the East and West fields are recorded which suggests that a two-field rotation was then practised.

Communal grazing practices, which may have an even longer history than arable farming, continue to the present day. For much of the medieval period they were organised through manorial courts, but now more frequently by moorland management committees. Woodland was also subject to common rights. Even today some common land used as cow pastures include relatively dense woodlands although one of the best examples, Rowleth Wood in Swaledale, has recently been enclosed by fencing. Many former cow pastures in Swaledale, between the low lying meadows and the moorland, are less wooded and were enclosed two or three centuries ago but sometimes names and scattered pollards, as at Arngill Wood on Ivelet Common Pasture, can provide clues to their location.

Communal control and co-operation was of great importance when arable fields and meadows were grazed by the animals of every farmer between harvest and sowing or stocking out and when fallow fields enabled all year round grazing and manuring. There was a need for grazing to be controlled or 'stinted' to ensure that the system was not abused by individuals grazing more than their fair share. Animals turned out onto a common pasture could freely

intermingle and thus all animals had to be clearly marked and identifiable by their owners and neighbours. 'Stints' or 'gates' were reviewed from time to time and fixed according to custom and need, but would originally have been allotted in proportion to the size of a land holding: as late as 1605 this pattern could be recognised in Braidley in Coverdale. Here tenants with 30 acres (12ha) had 16 beastgates (cattle) and 6 sheepgates, while tenants with 14 acres (5.6ha) had 8 beastgates and 3 sheepgates.

Fines were levied for such offences as overstocking, encroaching, or putting diseased animals on to the common pastures. Offending animals, particularly those straying off the common pastures or into arable fields were rounded up and placed in pounds or pinfolds where they would only be released on payment of a fine. Many townships still have a pound, a small stonewalled enclosure within or on the edge of the settlement. None is still in use, although some have been repaired with grants from the National Park Authority.

Communal sheepfolds, 'gathering pens', where sheep could be collected and separated into different ownerships, were another feature of communal grazing areas. The folds were often sited on the high moor (**51**) or on the edge of the common land. Some are still in use. Washed wool fetched a higher price at market and thus washfolds were sited close to easily dammed streams, where sheep could be washed a few days prior to clipping.

Despite the manorial courts, common land was constantly eroded by intaking and encroachment, particularly when there was not a strong lord of the manor. Piecemeal enclosure occurred throughout the medieval and early post-medieval periods by assarting: the reclamation of land from woodland or waste ground; by private exchange and purchase of strips in the common fields; and by the common assent of landowners. This process was mainly responsible for the network of small stone walled or hedged enclosures which surrounded most settlements by the eighteenth century.

51 A gathering pen on Surrender Ground, Reeth High Moor.

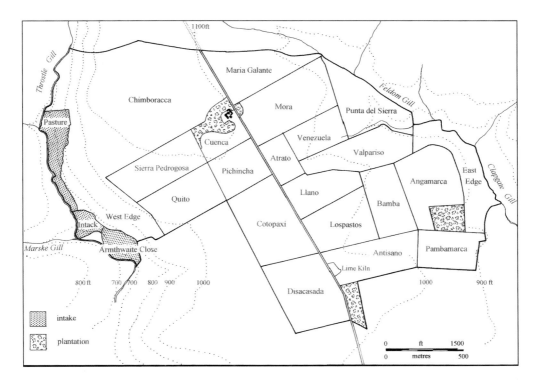

Parliamentary Enclosure

The century 1750 to 1850 was a great period of agricultural improvement in England, with a peak of activity towards the end of the Napoleonic wars. In the Dales improvement was most visible as Parliamentary Enclosure of the common grazing grounds or moorland, whereby common rights were extinguished in return for individual rights to allotments. The allotments could then be enclosed and improved or even sold. The main landowners in a township petitioned Parliament for most local Enclosure Acts. These large landowners would benefit, as they could afford the costs of building walls to enclose their newly apportioned holdings, and to improve pastures and stock breeds. Land improvement and reclamation generally involved paring and burning of the old surface vegetation, draining, and liming to reduce soil acidity.

Enclosure Commissioners, appointed under each Act, had the job of assessing the various common rights and then dividing the land up into separate lots or 'allotments' in the

52 Cordilleras Farm, Marske. A model farm laid out on newly enclosed land by John Hutton in 1809. The farm, and most of the fields, were named after South American mountains.

proportion of these rights, regularising the network of paths and roads and reserving small areas for communal quarrying. Most allotments were simply added to existing farms, but John Hutton of Marske Hall used most of the land allotted to him on the enclosure of Marske Moor in 1809 to create a new model farm, 'Cordilleras' **(52)**. Road making, walling, land reclamation, draining, and building the new three yard farmstead, was started in 1810 and by 1815 most of the farm was under cultivation. By the 1830s, however, most of the fields at Cordilleras had been put down to pasture. It now forms part of the Ministry of Defence's Catterick Training Area.

Walls and Hedges

Dry stone walls are the most extensive man-made feature in the Dales landscape. Many have been allowed to fall into disrepair as farms amalgamate or have been removed altogether to make larger fields, but more than 8000km (5000 miles) still existed in the National Park in 1988, together with 1000km (620 miles) of hedgerow and 250km (155 miles) of fence. A well-built wall should easily last for a century or more with little maintenance other than the replacement of loose topstones providing it is not subject to vibration or on an unstable slope. The oldest walls, now only visible as low earth-covered banks, date back to the first or second millenium BC. The alignment of these early walls has sometimes been preserved by later boundaries and field systems.

A comprehensive typology of existing walls in the Dales has yet to be prepared but variations in the appearance of walls can be recognised (**53**). Some of these relate to the underlying geology, others to the date of construction. Walls of the Parliamentary Enclosure period were often built according to a detailed specification laid out in an Enclosure Award. The 1778 Award for Fremington township specified that walls should be "seven quarters high (seven quarter

53 A contrast in walling styles at Fremington. The wall on the right is made of sandstone collected during field clearance. It formed part of the boundary of an area called Reels Head Intack which was described as 'ancient enclosures' in 1778 and is probably of early post-medieval origin. The wall on the left is made of quarried limestone and divides an area enclosed in 1778. It only has one row of projecting throughstones.

yards - 1.6m) exclusive of coap and coble (the two top courses) which said wall shall have two rows of throughs at proper distances and be made thirty inches (0.75m) wide at the bottom and taper gradually to 16 inches (0.4m) at the top..." Most walls had to be completed within twelve months of an Award. These enclosure walls were often built with stone from shallow quarries beside the walls. The majority of the arrow-straight field walls on the higher ground date from this period.

Earlier walls were more likely to have been built with stone collected from the adjoining fields: stone clearance was sometimes a factor determining the size of fields. A few probable medieval or early post-medieval walls can be recognised by their wide wall footings. These, often associated with large boulders or orthostats, often survive *in situ* even when the wall above has been rebuilt. Detailed survey of walls at Lower Winskill, in Ribblesdale, has identified lengths of narrow, nearly vertical, walls, built from stone apparently quarried from adjacent limestone outcrops, which have a coping extending over one face only. Documentary evidence suggests that these are early post-medieval or even older in date.

Enclosure walls were built in discrete lengths. Vertical joints or wall heads often indicate the responsibility of adjoining landowners for maintenance. These can sometime be mistaken for blocked gateways. Gateposts or 'stoups' were often made from large gritstone or sandstone blocks or stone flags. Before the widespread use of iron hinges and wooden gates, the stoups often had recessed slots or holes so that wooden rails could easily be lifted in and out of position as necessary.

Many field walls also contain sheep creeps, small rectangular openings at ground level which can be easily blocked, designed to manage the movement of animals between fields, particularly for access to water (**see colour plate 4**). Occasionally, passages can be found underneath roads and tracks. In some walls in valley bottoms similar openings prevent

'Forking holes'- small window-like openings high up on a gable or side wall enabled hay to be easily pitched up to first-floor level and also provided some light and ventilation. Ventilation might also be provided by narrow slit windows or by leaving open the putlog holes used for timber scaffolding during building.

The larger part of the barn is occupied by the hay 'mew' where loose hay was stored and used to feed cattle throughout the winter. The hay mew was filled up to roof level and on some barns might extend over the byre.

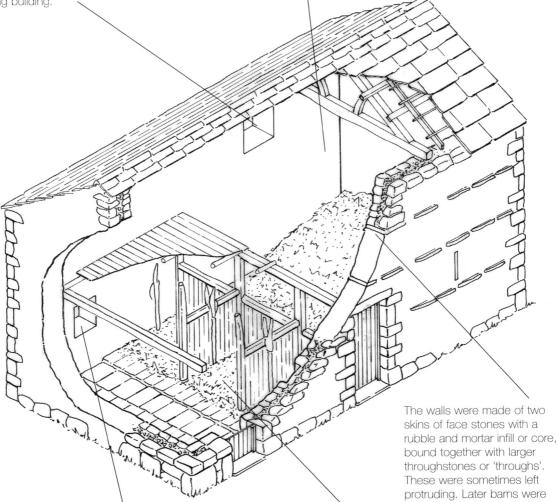

The walls were made of two skins of face stones with a rubble and mortar infill or core, bound together with larger throughstones or 'throughs'. These were sometimes left protruding. Later barns were built with lime mortar, but some early barns were of dry stone construction.

Manure which accumulated in a channel behind the stalls was periodically removed through the door or a secondary muck hole. A pile of manure just outside a field barn in winter is a good indication that it is still used.

The 'byre' where the cattle were housed was separated from the mew by a timber or stone partition. The cattle stalls usually had stone floors and were divided by timber or flagstone 'boskins'. Cattle were normally tethered to posts. Dialect names for the various parts of a field barn differed from dale to dale.

54 A typical Swaledale field barn, with separate entrances for the byre and hay mew.

a build-up of floodwater which might otherwise collapse the wall. Sometimes even smaller openings were built at ground level to encourage rabbits to use particular passages between fields and thus make them easier to catch.

The hay meadow - fieldbarn cycle

Fieldbarns, sometimes known as fieldhouses or cowhouses, were a particular response to the problems of overwintering stock in the relatively harsh environment of the Dales (**54**). The system revolved around grassland management. The most important components are the botanically rich hay meadows, but the system would not work without the extensive areas of fell grazing. In the spring, grass is encouraged to grow almost to seed in the hay meadows. Controlled grazing

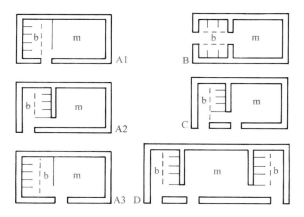

55 Typical barn plans of Swaledale and Arkengarthdale, recorded during a condition survey of 1044 field barns in the Swaledale and Arkengarthdale Conservation Area and classified according to the principal opening to the hay mew (m) and byre (b). Type A buildings have a single doorway located in a variety of positions. A1, with cattle stalled facing the gable wall, seems to be the earliest form, all the formerly thatched buildings having this arrangement. The commonest form, Type C, accounted for over 65% of the barns where the arrangements of the byre and hay mew could be identified. An extra doorway had been inserted into twenty-nine Type A barns to create a Type C arrangement.

and manuring in some traditionally managed meadows enables over thirty different plant species per square metre to flourish (**colour plate 14**). In July the grass is cut, traditionally with a scythe, and left to dry in the sun. Drying is hastened by occasional turning, formerly by hand but now with tractor drawn rakes. When dry the hay is swept up and stored in the barns. Sledges were used for hay transport on some steeper slopes as recently as the 1950s. During the summer and autumn the cattle graze the upland pastures but by November they are brought down and housed in the barns for the winter. Here they were visited by the farmer at least once, and sometimes as many as three times a day, to be fed and watered and, where necessary, milked. Six months later, in May, the cattle would be let out and the manure which had accumulated in the midden and byre spread back on the surrounding meadows to fertilise the next grass crop. Activity within the fieldbarn therefore varied through the year.

The true fieldbarn is part of an agricultural system which differs from the usual practice where farm activities start from, then gravitate back to, a central farmstead or farmyard and stackyard. With the fieldbarn system, instead of bringing hay from the meadows to farmstead buildings and transporting manure back to the fields in spring, the farmer walked around his barns in winter. This reduced the time taken to harvest the hay crop and substituted winter labour for spring and summer labour. Building barns in the corners of, or between, meadows minimised the transport of both hay and manure. A subsidiary effect on the landscape and settlement pattern is the comparative absence of farm buildings within many settlements in the upper dales, an absence accentuated by planning policies which have allowed barn conversions within settlements.

There are several thousand fieldbarns in the Dales. They differ in size, style and plan, generally being smaller on the poorer ground in the upper Dales. In Swaledale earlier barns tended to have a single opening serving both the byre and

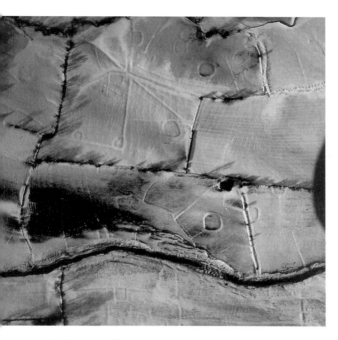

56 A group of rectangular and subrectangular stackstands, old field boundaries and drainage ditches near Countersett in Raydale. The snow cover has melted over part of the central field.

haymew and cattle stalled facing the gable wall. Most later barns had separate openings with the cattle facing an internal partition (**55**). Some barns had particular specialist roles. Nearly 10 per cent of the fieldbarns in Upper Swaledale and Arkengarthdale are for overwintering sheep, rather than cattle. Most of these hogg-houses (sheep are called hoggs between weaning and their first shearing) are single-storeyed buildings but around Muker there is a group of two-storey buildings, mainly sited on the fell edge. Sheep could gain access to the first floor direct from the moor while hay, swept up from the meadows below, was stored underneath.

The earliest dateable surviving fieldbarns are in the southern dales where several have seventeenth-century datestones. These tend to be larger than the cowhouses of Swaledale and Wensleydale and often have large cart doors and sometimes winnowing floors which suggests that they were used for the storage and processing of corn as well as for hay and cattle.

Just when stone fieldbarns became a common feature of the Dales landscape is unclear, but was probably nearly contemporary with the rebuilding of dwelling houses in the seventeenth century. In parts of Wensleydale and its side valleys are small ditched enclosures, generally more or less square in shape, slightly raised above the surrounding ground surface of meadows (**56**). These possibly preceded the widespread construction of fieldbarns. They are interpreted as stack stands which would have provided some security for stacks of hay, or perhaps for arable crops. Early seventeenth-century surveys of Wensleydale occasionally refer to fieldhouses, while recent fieldwork has also identified faint traces of a number of long narrow linear platforms which have been interpreted as the sites of wooden, cruck-built barns. The earliest reliably dated barn identified in a comprehensive survey of the 1,044 fieldbarns of Swaledale and Arkengarthdale is a much altered and extended barn near Ivelet dated to 1713. None of the Swaledale barns was of cruck construction but seventy-six had had their eaves raised at some stage, which suggests that they had once been heather thatched. Most were probably built, or rebuilt, between 1750 and 1850.

The small size of meadows and high density of fieldbarns in parts of Swaledale and Arkengarthdale has been linked to the practice of partible inheritance. This survived until the mid-seventeenth century. Property was divided between all children, not just the eldest son, leading to the sub-division of estates and a proliferation of small hay meadows and isolated cow houses. The pattern may also reflect the influence of industrial employment. Miners often sought to supplement their wages by working smallholdings, which would also provide some support for their families when mining was depressed.

7
'THE HILLS AFFORD GREAT STORE OF LEAD'

Lead mining, the most important extractive industry in the Dales, was a highly speculative activity. Miners could never be sure whether minerals would continue to be found in the vein they were working. Most veins are narrow, near-vertical, fissures in the surrounding 'country' rock. Lead ore, 'galena', is found either as distinct 'ribs' running through the vein or mixed with other 'gangue' minerals such as fluorspar, calcite and barytes. Occasionally copper and zinc ores were found in economic quantities. The richest veins were formed between beds of hard limestone or gritstone but a vein might be ore rich in one place and barren elsewhere in the same strata for no apparent reason. The industry centred on two main areas and most mining took place on moorland: few mines are found in the enclosed pastures and meadows (**57**). Its importance was recognised by the sixteenth century antiquarians, John Leland and William Camden. The chapter heading is a quotation from Camden.

It is not known when the mineral ores were first exploited. The composition of some early bronzes suggest that lead was deliberately added to this alloy. Excavations at Victoria Camp, an Iron Age settlement, found evidence for copper production. The Romans used lead for plumbing, roofing and coffins and finds of lead ingots or 'pigs' indicate an organised industry in the area shortly after the Conquest (**see 27**) but no definite early mining sites have been identified.

Apart from the Roman lead pigs there is little evidence for lead mining until after the Norman Conquest when documents indicate monastic involvement in the industry. Jervaulx Abbey was given the right to dig lead and iron ores in Wensleydale in 1145, although Count Alan kept the mines of Swaledale and Arkengarthdale. Roger de Mowbray's grant to Byland Abbey of iron ore throughout all his forest of Nidderdale included 'a tenth of his lead house'. This phrase

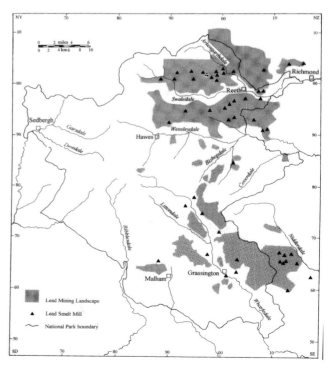

57 The principal lead-mining fields and smelt mills in the Yorkshire Dales.

suggests a well-organised industry with a royalty collected of one-tenth of the output of the mines. Fountains Abbey was given lead mines on the east side of Greenhow Hill. Large quantities of lead were needed for the roofs of the new monasteries and castles. Between 1179 and 1184, for example, some 700 tons of lead were shipped from Richmondshire for Waltham and Clairvaux Abbeys.

The field evidence for medieval mining is poor and the few documents which mention the industry are mostly concerned with production, boundary disputes, tolls and, occasionally, transport problems. Pack ponies were the main form of transport, especially in the more rugged areas, but wheeled vehicles were also used. The tolls on goods sold in Richmond market in 1307 included 2d on every cart load of lead. The Exchequer Accounts for 1365 include an entry for the hire of two wagons, each with ten oxen, employed in carrying twenty-four fothers of lead from Coldstones in Nidderdale 'by high and rocky mountains and miry roads' to Boroughbridge, for transhipment by boat to Windsor. A fother, like most medieval measurements, was determined by local standards, but typically weighed 21-22cwt (1066-1120kg).

Mining Techniques

Some lead ore probably came from secondary stream deposits but most early mining would have concentrated on veins visible at the surface using small pits, opencast trenches and shallow-shafts. Unfortunately, continued reworking of mining areas has removed most traces of early activity. The Romans knew of the technique of hushing. This could be used where veins were exposed on a hillside. The first stage was to collect water in a dam or a series of dams on the plateau above. Controlled rapid release of the water washed away soil and vegetation and may have helped to erode the country rock surrounding the veins, thus exposing the mineral and making it easier to extract. In most hushes, however, it is likely that human muscle power

was responsible for quarrying both the veins and the country rock and that water was mainly used to flush away debris or to assist in the dressing process.

The most impressive hushes can be found in Swaledale and Arkengarthdale where the mineral veins cross the side valleys (**see 6; front cover**) Turf Moor Hush, near Langthwaite, 400m (1300ft) long and up to 18m (60ft) deep, is one of the more accessible. It is dwarfed in size by the neighbouring Hungry Hushes, probably the wildest and most impressive mining landscape in northern England. The numerous earth dams here are minute in comparison with the worked area. Some hushes have shallow shafts dug into their floor or, as at Turf Moor, have been succeeded by levels, although at Lownathwaite hushing followed shallow shaft mining mapped in the late-eighteenth century.

Where a mineral vein was exposed at the surface, open trenches could be dug along the vein and spoil dumped on either side. Shallow shafts could be sunk to work at greater depths or through any overburden. The vein would be followed underground for as long as there was

58 A jack roller as illustrated in De Re Metallica, a textbook on mining and smelting by Georgius Agricola, published in Basle in 1556.

adequate ventilation in the mine or until the labour involved in hauling ore and waste back to the bottom of a shaft made sinking a new shaft more economic. Tallow candles provided both lighting and an indication of air quality. In primitive mines the ore and spoil would be carried in sacks up a ladder to the surface, but by the medieval period wooden buckets, 'kibbles', were lifted using a two-handed jack roller (**58**). Water could be brought to the surface the same way. Few shafts were sunk directly to a depth of more than 30m (100ft). This was because longer, stronger and therefore heavier ropes added to the weight of the bucket and its contents and made jack-rollers too difficult to use. However, greater depths could be worked by sinking shafts in steps within the mine.

Sometimes shaft mounds, commonly but inaccurately called bell pits, can be found regularly spaced approximately 30m (100ft) apart along a vein. In some townships an organised mining system was practised where the first person to discover a vein acquired the right to work it for two 'meres', while other miners could work the vein in adjacent meres. Traditionally, a 'mere' was the distance a hammer could be thrown but the spacing may also be linked with ventilation. This customary mining law is best recorded at Grassington and some boundary markers, 'mere stones', can still be seen on Grassington Moor (**59**). Regrettably, many others have been taken for private collections.

Underground, veins were worked in one of two ways (**60**). The main method was 'overhand' or 'overhead' stoping. Here, the miner worked the lead vein above his head, piling waste material beneath him to avoid hauling it to the surface. 'Underhand' stoping was also used. This involved the miner working a lead vein beneath him. Waste material was taken out of the mine or perhaps stacked overhead, supported on timber frameworks or drystone arching. In some later mines, hoppers were set into the sides of workings so that bouse, the mineral-rich material containing lead ore, could be shot straight into

59 Mere stone inscriptions from Grassington Moor, recorded by Dr Arthur Raistrick.

tubs. Blasting was never used for ore extraction, although gunpowder and, later, dynamite were used to help sink shafts and drive levels through the country rock and to widen veins.

As mines increased in depth so did drainage and haulage problems. These were partly solved by the development of new and improved techniques. The introduction of gunpowder made driving through unproductive rock viable and levels were introduced in the late seventeenth century, initially for drainage. This was a slow and costly process which required considerable faith from investors.

Veins were also worked by levels. Early levels were often little wider than the vein to minimise the amount of spoil that needed to be moved. Some levels were driven long distances into the hillside to intersect the position of known veins. The development of horse-drawn railways greatly eased underground transport and reduced the costs of bringing material to the surface. The remains of blacksmiths shops, stables and other buildings can be identified near many large levels. By the early nineteenth century horse levels were the main form of mining in the northern Dales, although where the topography was not suitable deep shafts were used.

Horse whims could lift water, ore or spoil from shafts over 100m (330ft) deep. Whims were wooden cylinders set on a vertical axis and turned by one or more horses. A rope wound round the drum ran over pulleys fixed on the shaft-head. The wooden structures of the whims have long since rotted away, but their position is sometimes marked by a flat platform, adjacent to a shaft, with a circular track worn around it, and large heaps of mining waste (**61**).

Steam engines were little used in the Dales for winding or drainage, unlike some other mining areas, although the engine installed at Cat Shaft, Hurst, in 1883, lifted coal for its own boiler, from a seam above the lead veins, as well as lead. Its rectangular chimney still survives, as does the neighbouring chimney at Browns Engine Shaft, installed four years later.

Water was an important resource and the hillsides above the main mining areas are scored with leats and dams. Water was used to provide power for winding, pumping, dressing and smelting, for ventilation and as a medium for

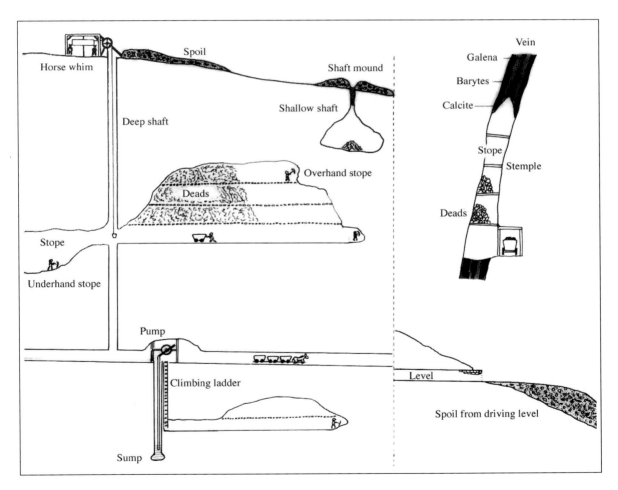

60 An idealised cross section through a lead mine showing underhand and overhand stoping, a horse level and a deep shaft with a horse whim. Inset - section through a worked vein.

dressing ore. The most complex water-management system was at Grassington. The total length of the principal leats here is over 11km (7 miles), with falls as little as 1:680. In the 1820s three dams were built across Blea Beck by John Taylor, the agent for the mineral lord, the Duke of Devonshire. Water from the dams was led across the moor in a clay-lined leat to another dam. Here it fed two large waterwheels. These powered pumping and winding operations, through a series of push rods, and later wire ropes, at a group of seven deep shafts

61 Spoil mounds from shallow and deep shafts along New Rake, Yarnbury. Near the centre is Wyatt's New Rake Shaft of 1827. Fingers of spoil radiate from the walled-up shaft, immediately above the circular track of the horse whim.

which are remarkable for their very large spoil heaps. From the waterwheels the Duke's Watercourse continued some 3.3km (2 miles) to Yarnbury to power a crushing mill built in 1824. In order to get the most from the scarce water another crusher was built, powered by the tail water. This in turn fed another two crushing mills at Beever and a pumping wheel before finally running into Hebden Gill.

Water could provide ventilation underground by being piped to the bottom of a shaft and discharged into a container which had small holes designed to allow air to escape. The water then drained away along a level. Occasionally underground waterwheels were used to pump water from lower levels and sumps. At Sir Francis Level in Gunnerside Gill, a waterwheel was used to compress air to power rock drills in

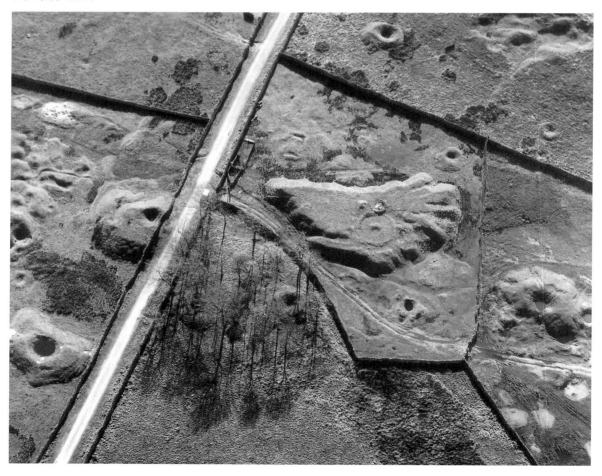

1870. Cast iron pipes also supplied water for a hydraulic pumping engine which still survives underground, as does the air receiver on the surface. Plans for a water-balanced railway incline in Gunnerside Gill, however, were never put into practice.

Dressing

Dressing was necessary to separate the lead ore from the gangue minerals. The initial sorting was carried out in the mine by keeping ore-rich material or 'bouse' separate from country rock. At the surface larger blocks of ore-rich rock would be hit with a spalling hammer and pieces of galena picked off by hand. This could be wasteful, but in the early days of the industry fine particles of ore were of little value as bale smelting needed large pieces of galena.

Smaller fragments could be retrieved by making use of the specific gravity of lead which is much higher than that of the other minerals with which lead is associated. If a mixture of ore-bearing rock is crushed to a uniform size, agitated and then allowed to settle in water, the lead ore will tend to settle before the less dense material. This principle could be harnessed to

separate small fragments of ore from sieved and crushed rock, using techniques similar to those of gold panners, by swilling on a shovel in a barrel of water or a stream. Finer material could be separated by buddling. This involved passing thin slurries of ore and water over a gently sloping floor or buddle. Lead ore settled at the higher end as the lighter material washed away.

Simple buddles were little more than rectangular wooden or stone troughs fed by a controlled flow of water, but from the eighteenth century the dressing process became increasingly mechanised. One advance was the hotching tub or jigger, a tray with a sieve base suspended in a water-filled tank. Lifting and lowering the tray allowed water to pulse through the sieve to agitate the material above it, thus allowing the heavier ore to sink to the bottom of the tray. At small mines 'buckers', small flat metal hammers, were still used to crush ore by hand, but at larger ventures water-powered mills with cast-iron rollers were used to crush ore, and banks of machines and settling tanks to separate mineral-rich material from the fine sands and slimes roller-crushing created (62). Waste could be reworked or discarded at each stage of the dressing process, so dumps below dressing

62 The Sir Francis Mine dressing floor on the west bank of Gunnerside Gill in 1900. A complex series of wooden launders supplied water to different stages of the dressing process, much of which took place in open sided sheds with corrugated iron roofs. Before the introduction of corrugated iron most dressing would have taken place in the open. Stream erosion has since destroyed much of this site.

floors often contain several different grades of spoil giving clues to the techniques involved. Bolton Park Mine is a good example of a small, late-nineteenth-century dressing floor. It operated between 1856 and 1872. The remains have recently been consolidated by the National Park Authority.

Bouse teams, found near the mouth of most levels, were open-sided bins where hand sorting could take place before suitable mineral was sent to the crushing plant. The number of bins gives an idea of the number of people working in a mine (**colour plate 15**).

Smelting

During the medieval period ore was converted to metallic lead using 'bales'. These simple bonfire-like furnaces used large quantities of wood for fuel and were probably responsible for much deforestation. Most were sited in relatively exposed positions on low hills or the brow of hillsides. Over seventy sites in Swaledale and Arkengarthdale have been located by the discovery of small quantities of slag and burnt stone or occasionally as placenames. At larger bale sites some slag may have been resmelted in blackwork ovens, using charcoal as fuel. Many bales were probably demolished after their last firing to recover any lead which had adhered to stones used in their construction. As the industry developed, smelting residues were often later removed for reprocessing in more advanced furnaces.

A map of the Copperthwaite area of Marrick, dating from c.1585, shows five bales. Four of these were just south of the Copperthwaite vein, apparently on Fremington Edge, while the fifth, *Priores Bale*, has been identified as a prominent hillock on Copperthwaite Moor. The name *Priores Bale*, more than fifty years after the dissolution of Marrick Priory, suggests that bales were either still used or very recently disused. Another c.1585 map shows a 'newe mill' at Marrick.

Ore hearth smelting was introduced in the late sixteenth century. The ore hearth, a small blast furnace with waterwheel-driven bellows, used a combination of peat and white coal (kiln

dried wood) for fuel. The first ore hearths were made of sandstone or gritstone but later iron castings were used. The hearth was about 600mm (2ft) square and 350mm (14in) deep with a projecting sloping ledge or workstone at the front. The charge, a mixture of lead ore and fuel known as 'brouse', floated upon the hearth and could be worked by the smelter. The hearths were normally raised above the ground and placed in an arched recess which supported a chimney. The arch provided working space for the smelter who would produce about a ton of lead in a working shift of about 10-12 hours (**colour plate 16; 63**). Early mills just had one hearth but by the late nineteenth century many mills had four hearths. The ore hearth produced large quantities of slag which still contained much metal. These slags could be resmelted on a slag hearth, often using coke as the principal fuel.

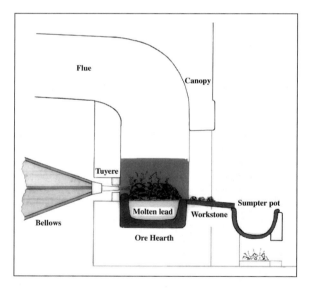

63 A section through an ore hearth. The smelter's skill lay in placing and moving the charge, a mixture of fuel and ore, on the cast iron hearth and controlling the temperature of the smelt with the bellows. At about 750° C, molten lead would flow down a shallow groove in the workstone into a separate sumpter pot. It could then be ladled or tapped into moulds to form ingots or 'pigs'.

Early mills had stumpy vertical chimneys but ground-level flues were introduced in the eighteenth century to take sulphur dioxide and other poisonous fumes away from the smelters. The realisation that considerable quantities of lead settled on the sides of flues led to the development of extensive flue systems. Some flues incorporated condenser houses and other chambers to increase turbulence and slow down the 'fume'. Side openings on most flues provided access for workers to enter the flue and scrape condensed 'fume' off the sides. These scrapings were sometimes flushed with water down to settling ponds. The flue system of the Grassington Moor smelt mill, the most elaborate

64 The base of a condenser house on the flue system from the Grassington Moor smelt mill. The lower part of the flue was dug into the ground, the upper part arched and covered with earth. The flagged floor enabled scrapings from the sides of the flue to be flushed down to settling ponds.

in the Dales, is over 1.8km (1970yd) long, includes two condenser houses and had two settling ponds (**64**).

More than eighty smelt mills are known from documents but only thirteen still have extensive above ground remains. The National Park Authority has initiated consolidation work on seven of these, including the Old Gang complex in Swaledale. As well as two smelt mills, this site has a large dressing floor and the remains of levels, hushes and shallow shafts. The larger, lower, mill, built in the mid-nineteenth century, had an internal water wheel, of which just the wheel pit remains. Four ore hearths were arranged in a row, with a smaller roasting hearth with a separate flue system attached in a separate building. The flues from the ore hearths utilise the rebuilt furnace arches of an earlier mill as a condensing chamber before merging into one 750m (820yd) long ground level flue. The main fuel used in the hearths was peat (**65**). A similar but smaller Peat Store can be seen 1.8km (1960yd) to the east at Surrender Mill (**66**).

Architecturally the most impressive smelt mill in the Dales was the Octagon Mill in Arkengarthdale. This eight-sided mill was built in 1804. Although initially successful, smelting was abandoned within a few years. The mill was reused as a sawmill and store, but partially collapsed in 1944. The hexagonal Powder House east of the CB Yard gives an idea of what was lost. The 'New Mill', built on the other side of the road in 1821/4, was more conventional in design (**67**).

The workforce

Much medieval mining may have been carried out on a part-time, perhaps seasonal basis, but the increase in scale instigated by development of new mining techniques, such as the use of levels, required both a larger workforce and investors. Although there were lodging houses at Old Gang in the seventeenth-century, most miners lived in the main Dales, walking to work each day. As the industry expanded short rows of small cottages were built in villages and hamlets such as Hebden, Grassington, Gunnerside, Keld and Booze to house the growing workforce. Some miners supplemented their income with smallholdings, such as the now-abandoned, small, isolated cottages surrounded by meadows and pastures, which can be seen in Kisdon gorge between Keld and Muker.

CB Yard (**68**) is one of the few groups of buildings constructed to house workers for the lead industry although it also contained another sawmill, stores and stables and homes for other estate employees. Greenhow Hill, a straggling group of cottages and smallholdings between Pateley Bridge and Grassington, is the only other settlement thought to have been deliberately founded to house miners. At the opposite end of the social spectrum the eighteenth-century Draycott Hall in Fremington, home of the mine-owning Denys family, is indicative of the wealth which mining produced.

Miners were likely to die younger than their contemporaries in other employment. This was mainly due to respiratory diseases, accentuated by living and working in badly ventilated damp or dusty conditions, rather than through accidents. Men, women and children worked on the dressing floors but the miners, smelters and mine agents were invariably male. In 1851, some 1,260 people were directly involved in the lead industry in Swaledale and Arkengarthdale as miners, smelters, ore dressers and washers out of a total population of 6,820.

The end of the industry

The lead industry in the Dales reached a peak in the mid-nineteenth century. It declined rapidly from the 1880s mainly due to falling prices as a result of the discovery of rich deposits overseas, forcing hundreds of families to try and find work in Durham, Lancashire and the West Riding or emigrate overseas. Houses and cottages were abandoned and fell into disrepair.

A few mines struggled on into the early twentieth century. These provided work for a handful of miners but many companies found that their machinery and buildings were their most valuable assets and sold them for scrap or

65 The 119m (391ft) long Peat Store at the Old Gang lead smelt mill reputedly held three years' fuel supply. It originally had a heather-thatched roof. The open sides aided wind-drying of the peat.

66 Surrender Mill, built in 1841, replaced two earlier mills on the site. It had three ore hearths and a slag hearth, powered by a central water wheel and bellows room. A roasting hearth was added later. Its flue, now some 750m (820yd) long, was extended in the 1850s but the fumes continued to pass through a chimney half way up the flue. The Coast to Coast walk crosses the flue just above the mill.

building materials. The furnace arches from the Old Gang smelt mill were sold for £25 in 1933 to the Muker Chapel stewards. The Octagon and New Mills were both bought by local builders shortly after the Second World War specifically as sources of dressed stone.

More recently some mine waste tips have been reworked and others used for surfacing tracks. The most extensive reworking has been on Grassington Moor. Here the Dales Chemical Company built a modern flotation plant, on the site of an earlier dressing floor, to extract fluorspar and barytes. At Old Gang, the Swaledale Mining Company put its machinery for extracting barytes from early dumps in the ruins of the lower smelt mill. The plant was later moved upstream into old removal lorries but

stopped work in 1992 and this site has now been cleared. All that now remains is the barren, silty mud in the tailings pond. The paths and tracks, initially built and maintained by the mining companies to get to and from their mines on the moors and often carefully graded, now provide footpaths and bridleways for the tourism industry. Some have been maintained and modified to provide access for grouse shooting and shepherding, often using crushed dressing waste for surfacing.

Lead mining has had a major effect on the landscape of the Yorkshire Dales. In 1993 English Heritage commissioned a map of the directly affected landscape as part of its Historic Landscapes initiative. The mapped area included the physical remains of lead mining: the mines, spoil heaps, smelt mills etc. and the immediately necessary infrastructure for their operation, such as water management systems. Wherever possible its boundaries followed physically recognisable mapped features. Some 400sq km (155sq miles) of the Dales was mapped as Mining Affected Landscape. Work has begun on defining the Mining Related Landscape: the area which was indirectly altered by the presence of mining. Possible indicators include population density

with large settlements containing small tenements, often at particularly high altitudes; small field sizes; and a large number of isolated field barns and trackways. However, other explanations for these can be suggested. For example, how much the pattern of small fields is due to miners supplementing their income with smallholdings, as well as being a reflection of agricultural activity, topography and tenurial history, is a current research problem.

67 The New Mill in Arkengarthdale, built in 1821-4. The water supply to the mill wheel passes through the roof of the T-shaped mill building. The building with the arched doorways was the peat store. The ruins of this mill complex were sold for building stone in the 1940s and today little remains other than the slag heap in the foreground.

68   The triangular shaped CB Yard and the remains of the Octagon and New Mills in Arkengarthdale. The flue from the six hearths of the Octagon Mill tunnelled under the Reeth-Tan Hill-Brough turnpike road to a short vertical chimney above the Hungry Hushes. The 'New Mill' later utilised much of the old flue. A complex series of tracks and water leats served the two mills and an adjacent saw mill. Below the outline of the Octagon mill is the spoil heap from the Old Smelt Mill Level, driven in the 1870s but abandoned before it was completed.

8
LEGACIES OF INDUSTRY

Today's pastoral landscape obscures the fact that the natural resources of the Dales provided the raw materials for a wide range of industrial activities. Although the evidence for quarrying, coal mining, iron making, and textile manufacture is now often slight, at times these industries were more important than the lead industry described in the previous chapter.

Quarrying

A handful of large quarries are now the only active heavy industry in the Dales. They produce surfacing stone for roads, aggregates for the construction industry and a limited amount of high quality limestone for the chemical and steel industries. Until the twentieth century, however, almost every village had at least one small quarry which provided stone for roofing and building purposes as well as more specialist uses. There are few accessible rock outcrops which have not been quarried, even rocks exposed at waterfalls such as Mill Gill, near Askrigg, have been worked.

Roofing slates and building stone

The sandstones of the Yoredale Series rocks provided building and roofing stone. In some places the sandstone lies in thin beds and can be easily split and cut into flags or roofing slates. In Wensleydale the industry expanded rapidly after rail transport provided easy access to the burgeoning towns of Lancashire and the West Riding. Most roofing stone came from

underground workings, like those at Burtersett, Gayle and High Abbotside (69). This avoided removing large quantities of overburden and the 'green' stone was also easier to work. Thicker beds provided stone flags for flooring and pavements. Some waste was used as walling stone, but the later extraction sites can be recognised easily by the grassed-over piles of thin waste near the mouths of levels. These are often approached by sunken tracks worn by the carts which took the dressed stone away. Most medieval quarries worked rock outcrops or shallow pits and these are harder to recognise, especially as markets were found for even the waste chippings.

The coarser Millstone Grit outcrops provided good quality gateposts and lintels and blocks were hollowed out to make stone troughs for watering stock. Some outcrops were also worked for the millstones used at the watermills found in many villages during the medieval period (70). Occasionally broken millstones or hollow scars where a stone has been successfully quarried can be found. Such scars often have an edge marked with narrow punch holes where the rock outcrop has been cut.

The hard, dark green-grey, mudstone flags of Horton in Ribblesdale, now crushed and used as a skid-resistant roadstone, used to be split and sawn to make cisterns and tanks for dairies and breweries. Other uses were for partitions between stalls in cowhouses and stables, gateposts, floor and roofing slates, tombstones,

boundary stones and shelves, especially in pantries and cheese rooms. A smaller quarry at the head of Crummackdale was famous for its whetstones.

Limestone

Limestone was widely quarried for building and walling stone. From the end of the seventeenth century to the early twentieth century some small quarries in Dentdale produced a polished limestone called Dent Marble, mainly for chimneypieces and monuments, but its main industrial use was as lime. Lime kilns, of various forms and in various states of repair are a common feature of the Dales. Most are small isolated drystone structures, mainly built between 1750 and 1850, sometimes freestanding but more often built partly into a hillside with a deep bowl at the top and a large, arched

69 The spoil heaps from old stone slate quarries form a level bench on the northern flank of Pen Hill in Wensleydale. A well-graded trackway zigzags up the hillside.

opening at the front (**see 5**). Within these kilns limestone, calcium carbonate, was burnt at about 900°C to make quicklime, using locally mined coal or sometimes wood and peat for fuel. Quicklime, calcium oxide, is unstable and reacts violently with water. This reaction could be harnessed to split rock in mining and quarrying. More often quicklime was slaked with water, under controlled conditions, to form lime, calcium hydroxide, widely used in buildings and farming. Lime was the main ingredient of mortars, plasters, limewashes and renders. Agriculturally it was used to improve or 'sweeten' grassland by reducing the acidity of hollow surrounded by a low bank. Few examples have so far been identified but more than 880 field kilns were mapped in the area of the National Park in the 1850s, mainly built by farmers to improve their own land. Although it was necessary to build the superstructure, field kilns were reusable and slightly more fuel efficient than both pye and sow kilns. Most were about 3.5m (12ft) high and built of limestone with a circular or near-circular bowl lined with sandstone or, later, firebricks which would not react with the limestone fill during burning (**71**). Variations in their design reflect local practice and date. Typical examples are square or circular in plan and have only one bowl and one, semi-circular, draw arch. Others have pointed draw arches or a series of stepped, recessed arches, while flat lintels were sometimes used on smaller kilns. Some later kilns, built for commercial production, had two or more bowls.

Kindling laid in the bottom of the kiln was covered with fist-sized lumps of limestone and coal. Much of the skill in lime burning lay in the careful tipping of layers of fuel and stone into the bowl. After about forty-eight hours, as the fire burnt through the fill, burnt lime could be

70 An unfinished millstone quarried from the millstone grit outcrop above Turf Moor Hush in Arkengarthdale. This was abandoned after splitting during the formation of the central hole.

pastures, especially of intake land and reclaimed moorland during the enclosures of the eighteenth and nineteenth centuries. Dead animals were often buried with quicklime to prevent the spread of diseases. Lime was also used in local industries, particularly as a flux in lead smelting and in tanning.

Lime-burning was a labour intensive process but the field kilns themselves represent a technology little changed from that of Roman times. Early kilns were essentially bonfire clamps: a piled up mixture of layers of limestone and fuel. These pye or sow kilns were destroyed after every firing to retrieve the lime. Thus their only remains are a slight circular or rectangular

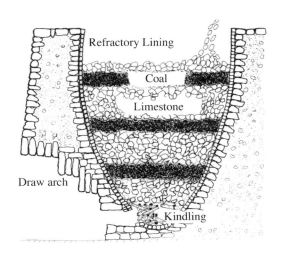

71 A cross section through a field lime kiln. Many kilns had simple draw arches instead of the stepped arch shown here.

shovelled out through the draw arch at the bottom of the kiln and more unburnt limestone and coal could be tipped in at the top, although it is likely that most field kilns were fired as an intermittent rather than a continuous process.

Most kilns are found close to small limestone quarries or limestone pavements, especially in areas of newly enclosed lands. A few were built alongside the Leeds and Liverpool Canal to take advantage of cheap coal. Rail transport led to large industrial kilns whose economies of scale led to the abandonment of most of the small lime kilns though some, especially in more isolated areas, continued in use until the early twentieth century.

Unlike the field lime kilns, two Hoffmann kilns, at Meal Bank Quarry, Ingleton and the Craven Lime Works at Langcliffe, operated on a horizontal principle. The massive Hoffmann kiln at Langcliffe was built in 1873 to take advantage of the new Settle and Carlisle Railway. This kiln consists of a series of 22 firing chambers forming a continuous tunnel when empty, in total 242m (795ft) long but arranged inside a 128m (420ft) long structure (**72**). Limestone from the quarry was brought to the kiln via a horse-drawn narrow-gauge tramway and carefully packed into the chambers. Coal, brought on the main railway line, was raised to the top of the kiln by a water balance hoist and dropped into the firing chambers through a series of feeder holes. The draught was controlled by a network of flues and a 69m (225ft) high central chimney. By opening and closing flues and controlling the fuel supply, one or two fires could be advanced around the kiln. The exhaust from these heated up the charge in the next chambers. Fresh limestone would continually be packed in the chambers in front of the burning zone and, after cooling, burnt lime forked out from chambers behind it and loaded into standard-gauge railway wagons in the adjacent bays. Hoffmann kilns were very fuel efficient and produced a very high quality lime but were labour intensive. The Langcliffe Hoffmann kiln was last worked in 1937. It has

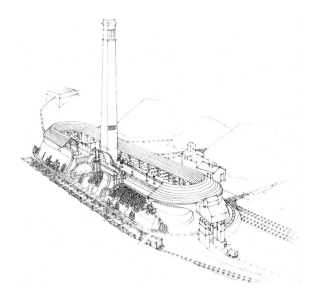

72 The Hoffman lime kiln at Craven Lime Works, Langcliffe. This continuous process kiln with 22 firing chambers was very fuel efficient but labour intensive. Built in 1873 to take advantage of the transport opportunities offered by the adjacent Settle and Carlisle Railway it represented the introduction of new lime burning technology and commercial enterprise.

recently been conserved by the National Park Authority, together with adjacent remains of a bank of three very large draw kilns, the stone abutments of a later vertical steel kiln, weighhouses and the tramway system.

Coal

Throughout the Dales there are numerous small coal mines wherever the thin coal seams of the Yoredale and Millstone Grit Series outcrop, despite the often poor quality of the coal. These were mainly worked from shallow shafts or levels. Some served individual farms or even just individual lime kilns, others provided coal for domestic purposes to neighbouring villages and towns. All that remains on most sites are access trackways, spoil heaps and, occasionally, the remains of a coke oven.

The Tan Hill area supplied coal to Richmond Castle in 1384 and was still worked as late as

1934. There are hundreds of grassed over shaft mounds but by the nineteenth century mining was mainly from deeper shafts, with horse power used for pumping and winding operations. Some shafts are still open and a hazard to unwary walkers. Trackways built across the overlying peat served the outlying shafts. During the eighteenth and nineteenth centuries much coal from this area was converted in primitive beehive ovens into coke, locally known as 'cinders', for use in lead smelting, particularly in slag hearths. Coke was much lighter to transport and had fewer impurities which would affect the quality of the lead (**73**). The account book of the mining agent Adam Barker shows that he was buying 'cinders' from Tan Hill for use at Old Gang as early as 1682.

The coal mines on Preston, Grinton and Redmire Moors were more extensive (**74**). The spoil heaps from shallow shaft mounds are scattered over some 6.5sq km (2.5sq miles). The industry flourished as chimneys replaced firehoods in domestic buildings from the sixteenth century. Lead was also worked here but the lead spoil heaps follow the line of the veins and contain more limestone and traces of minerals than the scattered, grassed-over, shaley coal tips. Winding was normally with a jack-roller. There were few buildings so there are few other above ground remains.

Some of the more visible remains of coal mining in the Yorkshire Dales can be found near Threshfield. These include the base for a steam winding engine and a washery built in the late nineteenth century to improve the quality of the coal. This was still a small-scale enterprise compared with the main coal mining areas of the country - the 1871 Census only records eight colliers at Threshfield. The route of a tramway which linked the mine with a limestone quarry at Skyrethorns and the Grassington railway can still be traced. West of the Craven Faults, around Ingleton, a group of deep mines exploited the thicker and better quality coal seams of the Coal Measures until the mid-twentieth century.

Iron

A medieval iron industry, stimulated by monastic enterprise, exploited thin bands of ironstone, mainly found in the Millstone Grit series. Easby Abbey had a share in a forge in Garsdale in 1250 and in 1281 the monks of Jervaulx Abbey were permitted by the Earl of Richmond to fell each year a part of their wood in Wensleydale and sell it or smelt iron with it at will. They could make two small sheds without nail, pin or wall to smelt their iron and if the smiths moved from one place to another they might make two other sheds as near as possible to their houses pulling down the first two. This description suggests a small itinerant bloomery industry, smelting ironstone in small clay furnaces with bowl-shaped bases sunk into the ground, using charcoal as a fuel and foot-powered bellows. The temperature in the furnace would be raised until much of the stony waste melted and ran off as slag, leaving a mass or bloom of impure wrought iron. The bloom was shaped and refined, with intermittent reheating, by hammering on a stone anvil to drive out any remaining slag and form usable bar iron.

By the fourteenth century water-powered furnaces which provided a stronger and steadier blast were in use. Remains of a late-medieval iron smelting industry have been identified in

73 This unusual coke oven survives high up on Fountains Fell in a coalmining field which flourished at the end of the eighteenth-century. It was built to provide fuel for the Malham zinc industry.

Bishopdale. Soon after the powerful Neville family had acquired the valley, an account roll of 1475 mentions the farm of Smelter, held by a William Irnman (Ironman). Neither this nor later accounts mention any income from

ironworking, which suggests that it had ceased by the 1470's. Towards the head of the valley, along leats running from the principal streams, fragmentary remains of a succession of water powered top-loaded furnaces, together with

74 The dense pattern of shaft mounds from coal mines on Preston Moor masks traces of earlier features. Lead mining is responsible for the lines of workings near the top of this aerial photograph.

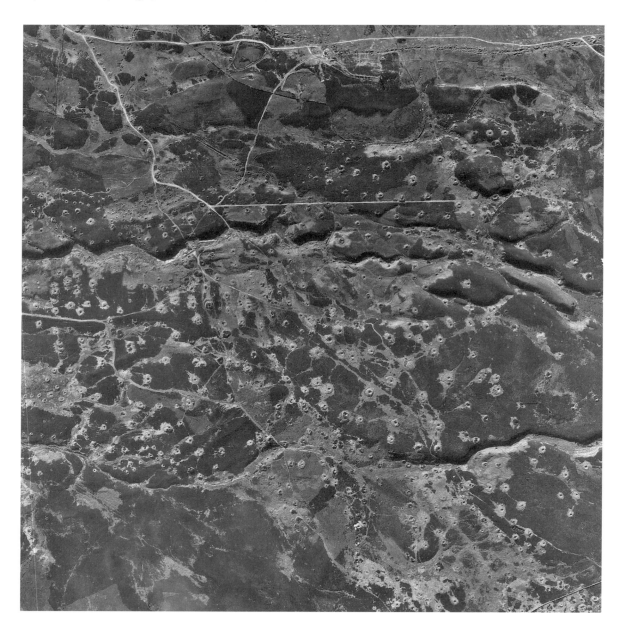

header tanks and forges have been identified. The sites are carefully located within bends in the streams to minimise the risk of damage from flood water. The scale of the iron working complexes suggests that the homes of a large workforce are waiting to be found in the valley.

It is not known why the iron industry disappeared. Exhaustion of the ironstone and bog ore deposits is one possibility, but it is more likely that the woodlands were unable to supply the vast quantities of charcoal necessary to keep continuously charged furnaces in operation. Conflict between foresters and and ironmakers was one of the causes of the decline of the iron industry in Skipton Chase. Foresters levied tolls on ore carried to the furnaces early in the fourteenth century, but in the 1320s iron smelting ceased for Barden and neighbouring woods 'had suffered grievous injury' from charcoal-burners and smelters.

Woodland industries

Many surviving broad-leaved woodlands contain evidence of being managed for the production of both charcoal and timber. Even when stone buildings replaced timber-framed houses, wood was still necessary for floors and roofs as well as numerous smaller structures and implements, and also as fuel. Different trees were managed for different specialist purposes. Woodland was a valuable resource in the medieval period and activities such as cutting timber or collecting brushwood were strictly controlled. Common rights still exist at Freeholders Wood near Aysgarth Falls, where coppicing has recently been reintroduced by the National Park Authority. Coppicing can be practised on most native hardwoods. It involves cutting a tree down to a stump at ground level. This, if carried out correctly, stimulates vigorous growth of new branches from the stump. These branches or poles can be harvested again after a few years and the cycle repeated.

Some coppice wood was converted to charcoal for iron smelting but the lead industry also consumed large quantities of 'chopwood' or 'white coal'. This kiln-dried wood was produced in small, oval, bowl-like structures 4-5m (12-16ft) in diameter. These are often partly built into a hillside and have a single opening on the downhill side. They are sometimes mistaken for small hut circles. Grass Wood, known to have been supplying chopwood to the Grassington smelt mills in the early eighteenth century, is one of several ancient woods in Wharfedale where 'chop kilns' or 'elling hearths' can be seen. The high cost of wood was probably one of the reasons why peat later became the main smelting fuel.

Ivelet Wood has been intensively surveyed to identify evidence for woodland management and industries. It contains at least six chop kilns and thirty-one charcoal burning platforms. Like many woods in Upper Swaledale it is subject to common grazing rights and thus it was not possible to practise efficient coppice management by enclosing compartments of the wood to protect regrowth from browsing stock. Instead, it appears to have been exploited on a haphazard basis. Growth ring analysis of charcoal from an excavated charcoal platform in the wood showed that much of the wood used in the last firing, probably in the seventeenth century, was over fifty years old, some over a hundred years old. Had coppicing been practised most of the wood would have been between twelve and twenty-five years old, depending on the length of the coppicing cycle.

Textiles

Much of the wealth of the monasteries came from their involvement in the textile industry - the accounts of Bolton Priory, for example, indicate the importance of wool sales and show that it was adding value by sorting and grading wool into different qualities. The introduction of water-powered fulling mills towards the end of the twelfth century encouraged development of the woollen industry in areas where wool and water power were readily available. Fullers are mentioned in Richmond at the beginning of the thirteenth century, while in 1394 Jervaulx

Abbey's tenant of their manor of Horton had to build two mills, one for corn and one for fulling. Clothiers from Richmond are recorded as trading as far afield as Westmorland, Coventry, Suffolk and London between 1385 and 1442. Spinning and weaving is likely to have been a widespread cottage industry, albeit much of it for domestic consumption.

The knitting industry which developed in the northern Dales concentrated on producing long woollen stockings. Seventeenth-century Swaledale inventories frequently mention small quantities of knitted stockings and wool. Knitting flourished because it was a suitable way of using the rather coarse local wool, because pastoral farming required little or no female or child labour except at haytime and, in Swaledale and Dentdale, because partible inheritance had led to numerous small family farms. The inhabitants of Richmond enjoyed a toll-free wool market and the trade flourished in the seventeenth and early eighteenth centuries.

There were several attempts in the late

75 Gayle Mill. This three-storey, six-bay mill was built as a cotton mill in 1784, with an internal waterwheel. It was converted to a woollen mill by 1804 and to a saw mill by 1872. In the centre is the wooden crane which lifted tree trunks to the saw bench at lower ground floor level. The wooden leat which supplied the turbine is on the left.

eighteenth century to introduce cotton manufacturing in the southern Dales and Wensleydale (**75**). Three water-powered cotton mills built between 1784 and 1785, at Aysgarth, Askrigg and Gayle in Wensleydale, did not flourish. This was due mainly to the difficulties of transporting raw cotton from the ports and the finished product back to the markets provided by developing industrial towns. The buildings were subsequently converted to woollen mills, while Gayle Mill was further converted into a saw mill in the 1870s. In 1879 its waterwheel was replaced by a water turbine, manufactured by the firm of Williamson Brothers in Kendal, which is believed to be the

76 The Burtersett candle factory has an unusual 'wrestler' ridge roof. The stone slates have been cut to form an interlocking ridge. Candles were the main form of lighting in the lead and stone mines.

oldest *in-situ* turbine in existence. This powered a large wooden rack saw bench and other woodworking machinery. The water supply to Gayle Mill is particularly ingenious. For most of the year the feed for the mill would come from a shallow weir built across Gayle Beck. When necessary, however, the beck flow could be increased by releasing water from a reservoir above the weir. The reservoir, which could be refilled while the mill was not working, could capture all the water flowing down the beck by means of a narrow rock-cut channel in the stream-bed. In the 1920s Gayle Mill, like many other Dales watermills, provided a public electricity supply to the village.

Many textile mills in the southern Dales were more successful, due in part to the easier communications offered by the Leeds and Liverpool Canal through Skipton and Gargrave. Langcliffe Mill, one of the first cotton mills to be built in 1783, was rebuilt in the early nineteenth century as a fourteen-bay, five-storey mill and a supplementary steam engine installed. A weaving shed, now the Watershed Centre, built 0.6km (650yards) downstream c.1840, reused the water supply from the mill. Most weaving sheds, however, were built closer to the parent mill. Some of the smaller textile mills failed in the mid-nineteenth century as their water power became insufficient for the developing textile machinery. One mill at Malham was labelled 'cotton mill in ruins' by the Ordnance Survey in 1847. The mill site, a small walled beckside enclosure, between the village and Malham Cove, had been given to Fountains Abbey 600 years earlier.

Most of the more successful textile mill complexes were built on the fringes of the Dales where they benefited from more reliable river flows and better communications. Lubricating oil from the carding machines and power looms, together with oils and dust from the wool and other raw fibres meant that fire was always a hazard for textile mills, especially those with wooden floors. Many mills have burnt down while others have been converted for alternative industrial uses or housing. Some mills were simply demolished, although their former presence may be indicated by rows of workers cottages.

Farfield Mill on the outskirts of Sedbergh, was the last textile mill still operating in the National Park. The first woollen mill here was built in 1836. A valuation of 1911 records a three-storey mill and an old two-storey mill. Other buildings in the complex included three two-storey warehouses, one of which contained a hand weaving room with seven handlooms, as well as a boiler house, a dyehouse, and various stables, storesheds and cottages. In 1940 the mill was requisitioned by the Government and used to make parts for aircraft. Woollen manufacture ceased in 1992 but part of the complex has since been restored by a local trust as a Heritage Centre.

Wool and cotton were not the only fibres used to make cloth. Flax was more widely grown for the production of linen before cotton became readily available. A survey of Grassington in 1603 shows that several tenants had small hemp plots attached to their houses. Somewhat surprisingly, silk was also manufactured in the Dales. A now-ruined, two-storey three-bay mill at Countersett, built c. 1800 for waste-silk spinning, combined ground floor living accommodation and an adjacent wheelhouse with a workshop on the first floor. Another possible silk mill at Burtersett was later used as a candle factory. Tallow candles made from animal fats would have been used in the local lead and stone industries as well as for domestic lighting. Despite the stream side location there is little evidence for the use of water power in this building (**76**).

Transport

The first major change to the route system that had developed in the medieval period was the introduction of turnpikes, privately financed toll roads, in the eighteenth century. The turnpikes were organised and financed through trusts, whose members were mainly local businessmen and gentry who hoped to gain returns on their investment through the tolls and from improved

business. The Richmond to Lancaster Turnpike Trust, formed in 1751, was followed by a trust for the Keighley to Kendal road two years later. Between Bainbridge and Gearstones, the Richmond to Lancaster road, which was 6yds (5.5m) wide, basically followed the line of the Roman road. In 1795, however, the long climb up Cam Fell was replaced by a route which passed through Hawes and along Widdale. Much of the old route is now an unsurfaced lane. Most of the early turnpikes in the Dales essentially followed and improved existing routes rather than creating totally new roads. A few were mainly new, such as the 1836 Richmond to Reeth road, a low-level route now followed by the B6270, which provided an alternative to a steeper route on the north side of the Swale through Marske. The now isolated roadside cottage at Haggs Gill, west of Ellerton Abbey, was a tollhouse for this road. Other surviving toll

77 A triangular milestone on the Grassington-Skipton road.

house buildings include a barn at Punchard Gate House, Arkengarthdale and a derelict cottage at Sandy Beck Bar, Rylstone. Milestones or cast iron mileposts can also be seen at intervals along

from Gargrave to Grassington was improved by the Duke of Devonshire to link with the canal to provide better access to his lead mines and enable coal to be brought in. This route was superceded in 1803 when the road from Cracoe to Skipton was turnpiked. The canal thus provided competition for the coal mines of Wharfedale, but it had little effect on the northern Dales. Problems with the water supply for the canal led to the construction of an impressive reservoir at Winterburn in 1893. This isolated reservoir has a spectacular 70m (76yd) long stone water ladder to take the overflow from the 175m (192yd) long dam, as well as a keeper's cottage. Other large reservoirs in the Dales were built to provide water for Bradford and other industrial towns of the West Riding. Their buildings and dams, such as those on Barden Moor, clearly show the confidence of the Victorian water engineers.

Railway lines reached the market towns on the fringes of the Dales between 1846 and 1862. These railways stimulated dairy farming and the tourist industry and led to various schemes for branches through the Dales. Only those to Grassington and along Wensleydale were built although a light railway, from Pateley Bridge to Angram, built to help construction of two large reservoirs in Upper Nidderdale, was open to passenger traffic between 1908 and 1929.

In 1869 the Midland Railway started building the Settle and Carlisle railway line as part of its own main line route to Scotland. This, the last navvy-built main line in Britain, involved construction of two long tunnels and four major viaducts. The best-known of these is the 400m (440yds) long Ribblehead Viaduct. The remains of the construction camps here, home to a changing group of workers between 1870 and 1875, can still be seen as low earthworks and flat building platforms (**78**). Not all the inhabitants of the camps were railway labourers. Building the railway demanded the skills of stonemasons, blacksmiths, carpenters, sawyers, bookkeepers, clerks and warehousemen. Many workers were also accompanied by their wives and children. Other camps existed at intervals along the line but have not yet been surveyed.

Most of the workers lived in prefabricated single-storey wooden terraces but the Batty Wife Hole settlement also included more substantial shops, public houses, a school, post office and reading room as well as a small isolation hospital built during a smallpox epidemic. Closer to Ribblehead viaduct lay the engineering camp of Sebastopol with its suburb, Belgravia. Sebastopol included a large brickworks, now marked by the stonework of its collapsed chimneys and piles of badly burnt waster bricks, as well as terraced lodging houses and an engine house with a sunken inspection pit. Stone for the piers of the viaduct was brought from quarries in Littledale along a narrow-gauge tramway, much of which is now used as a footpath.

A memorial to the navvies who died during construction of the railway hangs in the church at Chapel le Dale. Ribblehead station and other lineside buildings, more permanent structures than the wooden huts of the camps, were still being built after the railway had opened and most of the construction workforce had moved on. One hundred and twenty years later, the Settle and Carlisle route has been designated a Conservation Area in order to encourage the restoration of these distinctive Midland Railway style buildings. They are as much a part of the character of the line as the engineering achievements: the bridges, cuttings, embankments, tunnels and viaducts.

9
HALLS, HEARTHS AND HOMES

At first glance most buildings of the Yorkshire Dales are remarkably uniform. Roof materials are thin sandstone flags, locally known as 'slates', and wall materials are locally quarried stone, generally laid as roughly coursed rubble and occasionally rendered. Windows are small and, on older and unaltered houses, have dressed stone mullions and surrounds. Two-storey buildings are the norm. Some three-storey buildings can be found, but one-and-a-half-storeys with dormer windows are uncommon. Domestic, industrial and agricultural buildings are made of similar materials; domestic buildings being easily recognised by their chimneys and more numerous window openings. However, a closer inspection of this part of the cultural landscape shows a wide variety of detail and planforms resulting from the interaction of social and economic forces with both climate and geology.

Most buildings in the northern Dales use sandstone for both walls and roofs, although rocks from the different strata of the Yoredale Series are used for specific purposes. Coarser sandstones or gritstones are often used for lintels and dressings round doors and windows and for quoins at the corners of buildings. West of the Dent Fault, Sedbergh Blue Rag is common, but over much of the southern Dales the Great Scar Limestone is the dominant rock. This is less easily worked than sandstone or gritstone, but can be roughly shaped and used for rubble walling. It is less resistant to the weather so

benefits from a protective covering of limewash or lime render. Here, quoins and dressings are normally of sandstone or gritstone, with sandstone flags, or in Ribblesdale, Horton flags, used for roofs.

Although stone is now the dominant building material this was not always the case. Many early buildings were built of recyclable or perishable materials and the turves and clay used in most peasants' cottages have left few traces other than low earth mounds. Wooden posts placed directly in the ground would quickly decay, though rotting could be delayed by placing timbers on stone pads or stylobates. Stone can be recycled easily but this is only obvious when carved or dressed pieces are used. Pegholes and joint scars sometimes show that a timber was once in another building or roof. Buildings themselves can also be reused and have often changed both function and status over time.

Medieval buildings

There are few medieval buildings in the Yorkshire Dales. Those that have survived, other than the great castles and churches, either formed part of monastic estates or, like Nappa Hall, were the seat of minor gentry. This fortified manor house, built in 1459 by James Metcalfe, is a south facing single-storey hall between two towers. The high end is a four-storey tower with a turret, lit by slit vents, for a spiral staircase which ascends to the crenellated parapets (**79**). The tower retains its original windows but

79 Nappa Hall, a fine example of a fifteenth-century fortified manor house.

Georgian sash windows were inserted in the eighteenth century in the lower two-storey block which housed the kitchen and service rooms at the opposite end of the hall.

More impressive is Hellifield Peel, a large tower house built by Lawrence Hammerton c.1440. This had its own chapel in the southeast corner of the second floor. It was remodelled in the seventeenth-century and again in the eighteenth century when large Georgian windows were inserted in the north front. Grassington Old Hall is another rare survival. Two first-floor windows appear to be of late-thirteenth-century date, suggesting a first-floor hall. The remainder of the building, however, is a mixture of late-medieval, seventeenth-century and nineteenth-century features. Less obviously medieval is Fold Farmhouse, Kettlewell, outwardly a two-storeyed stone farmhouse of early-seventeenth-century date. Inside are the

remains of a late-fifteenth-century timber framed building. This was a four-bay open hall with a solar block to the north and a service end on the south. These ends did not survive its seventeenth-century rebuilding. However, enough remains of the decorative, smoke-blackened, roof structure of the hall, which originally had closed king-post trusses at either end and arch-braced collar trusses in between, to show that it was a high quality building, possibly originally a manor house. Kettlewell manor was bought in 1656 by a group of eight yeoman, the first Trust Lords of Kettlewell, who sold off the tenements and land but reserved the manorial rights for the benefit of the freeholders.

Timber, thatch and stone

These high-status medieval survivals tell us little about buildings at other levels of society. A few medieval and post-medieval accounts, surveys and inventories give some information about other buildings, and suggest that simple timber framed structures were once rather more common. In the most basic of these there was no distinction between wall and roof. The framework consisted of pairs of curved timbers, set in or on the ground, with their tops crossed and tied together with a ridge pole. Often the pairs of timbers were formed from a single tree, split down the middle. The lower part of these cruck buildings would be walled with brushwood and clay daub or perhaps with rubble infill and the upper part covered with thatch. Box-framed timber buildings, with mortice and tenon joints, have yet to be identified in the Dales.

In the twelfth century Robert de Gant granted Bridlington Priory the right to take wood (without felling trees) and wattles to make houses in Swaledale. In 1454, John Dytton reported to the Abbot of Dereham that he had 'paid for thakke (thatch) bought of T Rakys, and watlyng and thakking 2 houses entirely, viz, his said dwelling house in Ayrton (Airton) and the barn of the same house, 18s 4d. Also for drink given to the carpenters and for basyng the said houses, that is to say, for laying great stones (stylobates) under the foot of the Crokk, 4d'. Dytton was the vicar of Kirkby Malham.

No surviving cruck framed houses have been recognised in the Dales but a 1586 survey of Cracoe describes six farms, ranging from 14.5 to 34 ha (36 to 84 acres) in size, together with their buildings. All the farmhouses were of cruck construction, with either three or four pairs of crucks. Five had crucks of ash although the farm buildings had oak crucks. The houses appear to have been single storey but probably had storage lofts. A 'chamber on wall playtt' in one house may refer to an upstairs room. One of the houses, Coxon's Farm, was rebuilt in stone in 1669. Traces of curved principal roof timbers, continuing the cruck tradition, can sometimes be found, as at 41 Main Street, Sedbergh.

Cruck timbers reused as barn lintels, principal

rafters and purlins can occasionally be recognised, and a few cruck barns survive, the best-known being at Drebley on the Bolton Abbey estate. Traces of its former heather thatch can still be seen, protected by a temporary sheet roof.

Until the seventeenth century most houses and cottages would have been built with thatched roofs, generally with ling (heather) rather than straw, although a few higher status houses had stone slate roofs. In Swaledale thatch continued to be a common roofing material until the mid-eighteenth century (**80**).

80 Birks End, Swaledale. The steep gables of this small ruined two-cell direct entry house show that it had a thatched roof. The regular coursing of the stonework suggests that it was built in the early eighteenth century: if so, it is a late example of a heather thatched house.

Joseph Clarkson of Satron thatched his house in 1733 and his byres in 1734. In 1749 he slated the house but thatched the stables. Ling roofs had steep pitches, usually about 60°C, and the heather rested on closely spaced rafters which stretched from the top of the side walls to the ridge. This was often capped with turves pegged or tied to the thatch. A few lower status buildings, including some miners' cottages, were built with thatch roofs up to the mid-nineteenth century.

Fear of fire was probably one of the main reasons for reroofing in stone. Slating necessitated raising the eaves to flatten the roof pitch and strengthening or replacing the roof timbers to take the extra weight of the stone. It also increased the space available in the upper storey. Raised eaves lines can sometimes be seen in gable ends, especially on barns where they are less likely to have been rendered over, but often much of the gable was rebuilt. The pitch of a stone roof, shallower than that of thatched roofs, due to the heavy weight of the thin sandstone flags (2 - 2.5 ton per square metre) is normally about 35-40°c. The rafters support battens arranged to accommodate the courses which diminish in size towards the ridge. The slates were pegged onto the battens with split oak pegs, or sometimes sheep bone, driven through a hole in the top of the slate. The uneven surface between the slates on the underside of the roof was often sealed or 'torched' with mixtures of lime, hair, moss and clay to reduce draughts and penetration of rain and snow.

Plan forms

Cruck construction produced simple cellular buildings. The length of a cruck framed house could be extended indefinitely by adding pairs of crucks, but height and width were restricted by the size of available timbers. The entrance could be through a gable wall or a long elevation. The variations in ground plan form in surviving vernacular houses basically depend on the relationships between the positions of the main entrance, the main hearth or fireplace and the position of the rooms. Although houses have

often been subjected to considerable rebuilding and remodelling, some plan form elements may be fairly reliably detected from outside. The main door and the main chimney are usually still in use. Often only the main room, variously called the hall, housebody, firehouse and forehouse, was heated. Small openings, 'fire windows', on one or both sides of the principal fireplace may indicate its position. Staircases are usually less obvious unless lit by a window at a half-landing or contained within a projecting bay. Conventionally, the 'upper' end of a house contains the more private rooms, while the 'lower' end contained the kitchen and services. Where a house is built across a slope the 'lower' end is normally downslope. This probably reflects the practice found in longhouses where the animals would be housed below the cross-passage to prevent manure seeping into the housebody.

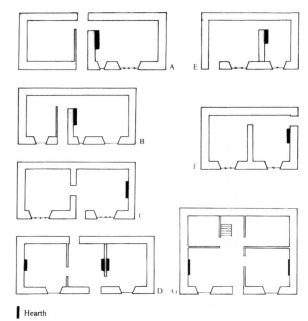

Hearth

81 Some typical plan forms of vernacular houses. A - longhouse with people and animals using the same entrance passage. No surviving examples of this type have yet been found in the Dales. B - two-cell with cross passage. C - two-cell direct entry, end fireplace. D - three-cell central lobby. E - two cell end entry, axial fireplace. F - two-cell gable entry. G - double-pile house.

The basic two-unit plan of the simplest houses in the Dales has a living room and kitchen on the ground floor and bedrooms or a loft above (**81**). The practice of partible inheritance in Swaledale may have encouraged the development of two-cell buildings with central entry and end chimney which could be easily subdivided into two dwellings. This popularity of this plan could also stem from the practice of rebuilding one side of a cross-passage house at a time. True double-pile plans, where the width of the house was increased, first appear in the seventeenth century although wider ground floor plans had been achieved with an outshot. Old Hall, Thoralby, dated 1641, is one of the earliest double-pile houses in the Dales.

Rebuilding in stone

There are few medieval houses, but there is a wealth of buildings dating from the seventeenth century, particularly higher-status houses. After the Dissolution of the Monasteries and the political upheavals of the sixteenth century a new class of tenant and freehold farmers developed. The growth of the butter market with London, the production of knitted woollen stockings, mainly for export to Germany and the Low Countries, and expansion of the lead industry all combined to create prosperity, some of which was consumed in improved housing. In general, the houses of the gentry were rebuilt first, followed after the Civil War of 1640-9, by some of the more independent farmers. Perhaps the most prominent example of a gentry house is Friars Head, Winterburn, a three-storeyed house built by Stephen Proctor c.1590. His family had been tenants of Fountains Abbey before the Dissolution (**82**).

The date of rebuilding varies from dale to dale, reflecting local circumstances as well as

82 Friar's Head, Winterburn. The projecting bays of this imposing late-Tudor house each have 6-light mullion and transom windows and three-light ogee headed windows in the gables.

fashion. Several farmhouses in Bishopdale, for example, were rebuilt to a particularly high standard before the Civil War, while there was little rebuilding in the Sedbergh area until the eighteenth century. The popularity of rebuilding houses with two or more storeys was helped by the more widespread use of lime mortar. Using lime mortar aided the construction of load-bearing walls. Lime had been known to medieval builders but previously had been rarely used in vernacular buildings, perhaps because of its cost.

The hearth tax levied in the mid-seventeenth century provides details of the number of hearths in each house and is thus an indication of size and prosperity. Over a third of all houses in the Craven area had more than one hearth in 1672-3. Datestones on surviving buildings suggest that many of these were built in the third quarter of the seventeenth century and, while dates before 1650 are rare, stylistic evidence suggests that there are more early-seventeenth-century buildings than in Wensleydale and Swaledale. Most Craven houses were built on a two- or three-cell plan although there are several examples of more complex plans, particularly amongst the earlier buildings. Numerous variations of fireplace and entrance positions can be found.

A particular feature of Craven farmhouses is a two-storey porch, often added shortly after the main house was completed (**83**). The porch at Foxup House, a small farm at the head of Littondale, dated 1673, is large enough to include a small dairy and a chamber on the first floor. In many Craven houses considerable attention was paid to the status symbol of external decorative detail although internal decoration tended to be less lavish. Carved doorheads with doorways framed with heavy quoined jambs are particularly rich in the Settle area.

Three storeys were another status symbol, although these were restricted initially to the houses of the minor gentry such as Kilnsey Old Hall. Here, a datestone with the initials *CW* and date *1648* refer to Christopher Wade who constructed the present building, incorporating

earlier walling which was probably part of the Fountains Abbey grange. His rebuilt house, unusually for the period, had the hall and parlour at first-floor level, entered by steps from a cross-passage. The floors were removed when the house was converted for agricultural use and a large arched doorway inserted into the north wall, but the fireplaces and traces of a decorative plaster frieze remain. The attic above the north-west wing contains a pigeon loft with stone nesting-boxes in all four walls. Traces of a decorative chequerboard render survive on the west elevation. Lady Anne Clifford stayed here in 1663, en route from Skipton to Pendragon Castle. After 1693 the Hall was let to tenants and became a farmbuilding sometime in the nineteenth century. It was converted back into a private house in 2000. Renards Close Laithe, a field barn 450m (490yds) south-west of the Hall shows that the Wades invested in their estate. It has a lintel inscribed *CW1661* and reused cruck timbers.

Much of the new seventeenth-century housing initially combined vernacular elements such as timber firehoods, a single-depth plan and sometimes a cross-passage as well, with features such as mullioned windows which were made fashionable during the Elizabethan and Jacobean gentry rebuilding. The windows were normally deeply recessed and often had three or more lights in the main rooms of the house. Sometimes, particularly on grander houses, the mullions were divided by transoms as at Coleby Hall in Wensleydale. Square headed windows were the norm, usually hooded with horizontal moulding designed to keep rainwater from dripping onto the glazing. Sometimes three-light windows were stepped, the centre light raised above the others and paralleled by the hood. Occasionally however there were round-headed windows, as seen on the fire windows at Oxnop Hall near Muker. The two-storey porch here has a lintel inscribed *FIA 1685*.

Mullions are found in various profiles but like other decorative detail in the Dales only provide an indication of date. Oak mullions were

common in the western Dales where there was little access to sandstone. Hollow chamfered stone mullions tend to be earlier than those with splay or ogee profiles but in a few houses flush square-section mullions, normally associated with eighteenth-century buildings, and simple moulded frames were being used before the end of the seventeenth century. Stone mullions became unfashionable in the 1720s and were replaced by small rectangular windows with

83 This fine porch at Eshton Manor Farm has jettied stone corbels supporting the first floor, a stepped three-light window and gable coping with finials on top of the kneelers.

sliding casements. Sash windows became the norm towards the end of the eighteenth century.

Usually only the chimney stacks can be seen but on some early buildings large external stacks were attached to a gable (**84**). Most chimney stacks are rectangular and built in dressed or roughly dressed stone, but in the northwestern Dales cylindrical rubble stone stacks sometimes advertise the presence and status of heated rooms. High Hall, Dent is perhaps the best example. Dated 1625, it had two massive end chimneys, topped with cylindrical stacks. A third gable chimney, added when the building was extended in 1664, has a rectangular stack. Some contemporary buildings still continued to be built with timber and plaster firehoods, particularly for the principal or cooking hearth. Stone-arched fireplaces became a feature of many larger farmhouses between 1620 and 1710, often with large shaped voussoirs, or sometimes with huge stones scribed in imitation.

The dates on door lintels suggest the major building or rebuilding boom in Swaledale and Wensleydale occurred slightly later than in Craven. Detailed surveys suggest that the new buildings bore little resemblance to any that had previously existed. Many houses are of similar size and, in contrast to Craven, the Hearth Tax returns for 1672-3 show that less than a quarter had more than one hearth.

Mid-seventeenth-century builders used a variety of plan forms (**see 81**). In the village of Thoralby are houses built with hearth passage, double-pile, two-cell direct entry and three-cell direct entry with axial chimney stack ground floor plans. Contemporary examples of houses with central and end lobby layouts can be found within a few kilometres. The direct entry plan gradually became the most common. Most three-cell houses usually had a direct entrance into the hall with the hall fireplace sharing a chimney stack with the parlour beyond. The third room at the other end of the building was used as a second parlour or as a service end.

No true longhouses, that is, buildings used by both humans and livestock and entered through a common passage, are known in the Dales but there are several examples of cow byres and houses under the same roof line. The door lintel

84 Glebe Farm, Thornton in Lonsdale has large external chimney stacks on both gables but only one survives above eaves height.

of New House in Bishopdale shows it was built for Christopher Clough and his wife Elizabeth in 1635. When built it would have been thatched, for a former steep-pitched roof line can be seen in the rubble wall of the east gable. The house, which has three ground-floor rooms, has an entrance lobby beside the chimney stack between the housebody and the east parlour. The cow byre and barn are later additions (**85**).

Polite architecture

There are several more polite buildings which owe little to vernacular traditions. One of the earliest polite buildings in the Dales to use ashlar stonework (regularly coursed sawn stone blocks) is the Fountaine Hospital in Linton, a group of six almshouses surrounding a chapel c.1721. Its influence can be traced locally in rebuilds of Linton House and Old Hall House as well as in some farmhouses in surrounding villages. Many of the larger country houses reflect national fashions and the wealth of their owners, often derived from interests outside the

Dales. Some were built as the homes of local gentry, others to provide seasonal accommodation, particularly in connection with the sport of grouse shooting which was developing in the late-eighteenth and early-nineteenth centuries. Marske Hall, home of the Hutton family, was begun c.1597 and rebuilt and extended in classical style c.1730. The estate includes a c.1750 quadrangular stable block and an early-nineteenth-century range of farmbuildings and is surrounded by formal landscaped gardens. Grinton Lodge, now a Youth Hostel, was built for James Fenten in the early nineteenth century as a shooting lodge. The Erle-Drax family of Charborough House, Dorset, who built a regency villa at Ellerton Abbey c.1830, probably created a romantic ruin from the remains of the mainly fifteenth-century tower of the Cistercian nunnery at the same time. The formal gardens to the west of the house included a small lake, reusing part of a monastic feature. Some of the other earthworks here are the remains of a deserted medieval settlement.

85 New House, Bishopdale, the earliest dated house in the valley.

86 The east front of Swinithwaite Hall. The house may be of seventeenth century origin but was modified by John Foss of Richmond for T. J. Anderson in the second half of the eighteenth century.

Swinithwaite Hall was rebuilt to the design of Richmond architect John Foss c.1795 (**86**). Foss also designed the two-storey summerhouse by Temple Farm and may also have been responsible for some farm buildings on the Swinithwaite Estate. Many of the larger houses are on the fringes of the Dales, reflecting both richer agricultural land and better access to urban centres. George Webster of Kendal remodelled several country houses in the first half of the nineteenth century including Ingmire Hall at Sedbergh in a Tudor Gothic style, and Eshton Hall and Flasby Hall in an Italianate style. Ingleborough Hall was remodelled in a Greek Revival style for the Farrer family c.1814. Like many contemporary houses it has an icehouse, but more unusually the grounds include tunnelled paths to keep servants and agricultural traffic out of sight from the house. Even odder are the follies built for Mrs Hutton in the grounds of Sorrelyskes in Bishopdale in the mid-

nineteenth century: a cone with large stone fins like a rocket on a launching pad, a narrow waisted 'pepper pot' and the complete facade of a chapel, which included a blank Gothic arch and a bull's eye window.

Industrial growth

Expansion of the mining and textile industries in the eighteenth and nineteenth centuries increased the demand for housing. Some of this was met by subdivision and extension of existing houses, particularly by the addition of an extra bay or bays, but rows of small terraced cottages developed on the edges of settlements in the mining areas and near the larger textile mills (**87**). These were built of local materials and thus add only differences in scale and density to the appearance of villages. Most surviving examples are two-storeyed and stone-roofed, following the building techniques developed in the preceding centuries, and often had only one bay with a direct entry into the parlour and a small outshot at the back for a pantry. A few miner's cottages at Hurst, single-storey and thatched, were recognised as being amongst the worst dwellings in Swaledale in 1841.

87 A row of former miner's cottages at Hurst. Although modernised, its symmetry has not been spoilt by incongruous plastic windows.

88 The eighteenth century Wesleyan Chapel in Reeth was rebuilt in 1822 and given a more imposing facade in 1840. The round headed windows were only installed c.1907. The chapel still retains its gallery and pews.

New building styles developed with the introduction of the railways, which brought different building materials into the area. This is most noticeable along the Settle and Carlisle railway line, where the lineside buildings, particularly the stations, station masters' houses and railway workers' cottages are in the Midland Railway's 'Derby-gothic' style, an early form of corporate branding. The pattern book designs, originating from the company architect, J.H. Sanders, include decorative details such as arched headed windows, slate roofs with special crested ridge tiles for the single-storey station buildings and stationmasters' houses, prominent gables with broad overhanging eaves, and distinctive bargeboards. The workers' cottages, normally built in terraces of four or six, are simpler but had more generous proportions than most miners' cottages. The roofs of Welsh slates were cheaper and lighter than the local stone flags. In the late nineteenth century speculative villas were also constructed near to some stations, for example at Grassington, Sedbergh and Hawes, where the railways offered commuting or business opportunities.

A range of social buildings were constructed in most villages during the nineteenth century. Early Quakers and Nonconformists had met in houses and barns but as their congregations grew so did the need for dedicated places of worship. Most meeting houses and chapels at first were simple functional buildings, built by voluntary labour (**88**). Some later chapels were much larger, such as the Wesleyan Methodist chapel at Gunnerside, rebuilt in an Italianate style in 1866-7 with seating for 300 in the gallery and 400 on the ground floor. Many villages had two or more Nonconformist chapels, each dedicated to a separate sect, but most have since been converted to other uses, often to housing. Similar community initiatives, and a desire for self-improvement or perhaps for recreation not linked to alehouses, led to the development of reading rooms. Fifty-three reading rooms and literary institutes have now been identified in the Yorkshire Dales, ranging

from simple corrugated iron structures to architect designed halls. Schools, many also funded through voluntary subscriptions, were built in most villages, continuing a tradition which had begun with the foundation of grammar schools at Burnsall and Askrigg in the early seventeenth century. Most of the small village schools have now closed and been converted to outdoor centres, surgeries or, more often, houses.

The population decline as a result of the collapse of the mining industry meant that there was relatively little new building in the early twentieth century: the number of houses fell as buildings were abandoned and fell into disrepair or were joined together to form larger homes. After the First World War depressed land prices, rising living standards and transport innovations led to prefabricated timber-framed bungalows being erected as weekend retreats, particularly in Chapel le Dale and Littondale (**89**).

Local authority housing, using standardised designs and materials, concentrated on some of the larger villages, either as ribbon development or around small 'greens'. In a few villages there are small speculative housing estates, often partly faced with natural stone but otherwise bearing little relationship to the character and form of existing settlements.

For most of the second half of the twentieth century, planning control has meant that the majority of new housing has been limited to barn conversions, infilling on vacant plots within villages or the construction of houses and bungalows for farmers and other agricultural workers. In the late 1980s national relaxations on control over mobile homes effectively permitted a new village to develop, in ancient woodland, at Long Ashes at Threshfield. This is a successor to the weekend retreats of the 1920's, but the chalet building styles, artificial materials and suburbanised gardens add very little to their surroundings. Overall, however, the conservation movement and planning control have helped to ensure the survival of traditional buildings and the use of local materials.

89 An escape from the city? A small prefabricated
timber bungalow set amongst meadows close to the
River Skirfare in Littondale.

10
A PAST FOR THE FUTURE?

In 1954 part of the Yorkshire Dales was designated a National Park. Adjoining areas, the North Pennines, the Forest of Bowland, and Nidderdale, have since been designated Areas of Outstanding Natural Beauty in recognition of the importance of their landscapes.

The National Park aims are to 'conserve and enhance the natural beauty, wildlife and cultural heritage' and to 'promote opportunities for the understanding and enjoyment of the special qualities of the park by the public' while supporting the economic life of the community. The National Park Authority, an independent body run by county and district councillors and members appointed by the Secretary of State to represent both national and parish interests, works through a mixture of advice, control, incentive and direct intervention. It designates Conservation Areas and controls some development through the town and country planning process although its planning powers are little stronger than of other rural areas.

National Park staff provide technical and professional advice, ranging from how to make best use of agricultural grants to techniques of pointing buildings. The Area Management Teams, helped by groups of volunteers, maintain the rights of way network of footpaths and bridleways. The National Park Centres in each of the main dales, the Dales Countryside Museum, guided walks, Explore and Discover events, lectures and publications, the latter ranging from children's activity leaflets to self-guided walks

and technical papers, are all intended to help people interpret, appreciate and understand the landscape of the Yorkshire Dales. Practical conservation measures are encouraged by offering a range of grants and management agreements to householders, farmers, parish councils and other landowners. These include a Barns and Walls Conservation Scheme which, utilising resources from English Heritage, central government and European sources, offers capital grants for the repair and maintenance of fieldbarns and walls. Over £2m worth of work was carried out as a direct result of this scheme between 1989 and 2001. A Local Historical Features project offered up to 100 per cent grants for the consolidation of a wide range of small man-made features, such as lime kilns, pounds and sheepfolds, which help produce the cultural character of the landscape. Management agreements and a whole Farm Conservation Scheme are amongst other tools which help protect what is important about the Dales landscape.

Few archeological sites in the Yorkshire Dales have been excavated and even fewer have been excavated using modern scientific techniques. Archaeologists' ability to gain information about the past through scientific investigation is improving every year, so today sites are only excavated as a result of unavoidable development threats or to resolve very specific research questions which cannot be answered in any other way. This is partly because excavation

90 Detailed topographical survey in progress at merrick Priory, in advance of redevelopment proposals for the farm and the outdoor centre which occupy the site of the medieval nunnery.

is an expensive, time-consuming process, but also because it effectively destroys the archeological resource and thus makes it unavailable for future investigation. The National Park Authority tries to avert development threats, but it does encourage and support well founded research.

Many of the archeological sites featured in this book have benefited from survey organised or supported by the National Park (**90**). Projects range from supporting university-based research into the nature of the Mesolithic hunter-gatherer economy to commissioning detailed survey by professional archaeologists of the construction camps of Ribblehead Viaduct. More sites continue to be discovered each year, often as a result of the work of amateur archaeologists. Some of these workers are also recording known sites in greater detail or trawling through

historical records which help explain the development of the landscape. The results of such projects are all detailed in the Sites and Monuments Record. This now contains over 25,000 records of archeological sites.

Many of the survey projects supported have been specifically aimed at improving the management of archeological sites. These range from the production of measured drawings of the buildings of lead smelt mills and other structures where consolidation work is planned, to less intensive identification surveys of farms or groups of farms subject to management agreements. These surveys identify the presence of archeological and historical features so that agreed farming practices can take the archaeology into account.

The National Park Authority is one of many agencies involved in the management of the Dales landscape. The Authority set up the Yorkshire Dales Millennium Trust in 1996 to access lottery funding and other alternative funding sources in order to provide grants for conservation purposes. English Heritage provides grants and technical advice and advises central government on the designation of historic buildings and Scheduled Ancient Monuments. English Nature has a specific responsibility for the scientific conservation of plants and animals, designates National Nature Reserves and Sites of Special Scientific Interest and offers management agreements to protect species and habitats, most of which also protect archeological interests. The National Trust has an estate centred on Malham and Upper Wharfedale. However, relatively little land is publicly owned, most of it is cared for by private owners.

The 1949 National Parks and Access to the Countryside Act which provided the statutory framework for national parks did not foresee any conflict between the interests of agriculture and conservation but for many years government policies aimed at maximising agricultural production failed to take account the impact on the landscape. Change was encouraged by giving grants to plough and re-seed hay meadows with grasses which relied on chemical fertilisers rather than traditional manure; to drain moorland; to build large new farmbuildings, silage clamps and agricultural roads, and to rip up hedges and walls. Forestry concentrated on various species of pine, particularly lodgepole pine, douglas fir, larch and spruce rather than native hardwoods. In the 1980's policies began to change and parts of the higher dales, where more traditional farming techniques had survived, were incorporated into the Pennine Dales Environmentally Sensitive Area. Here farmers who enter into voluntary management agreements receive payments in return for practising less intensive agriculture and thus maintaining the hay meadow and field barn landscape. The ESA and a similar agri-environment scheme, Countryside Stewardship, were superceded in 2005 by Environmental Stewardship. This whole farm scheme open to all farmers requires environmental assets on the farm to be assessed and provides support for conservation friendly farming.

Intensification and mechanisation was accompanied by a decline in the number of people working on the land and increased the pressure on those who continue. Small farms amalgamated, resulting in larger flocks and herds and fewer hands to maintain walls and barns. These consequently fell into disrepair and were abandoned or sold for building materials. Many farmhouses and cottages are now used in the growing tourism industry, either as second homes or as holiday homes, resulting in seasonal pressures on local services, and, indirectly, to the closure of village shops and schools.

Other threats to the landscape of the National Park include demands for new housing, particularly low cost housing, commercial pressure for use of standardised materials and structures, whether in buildings or transport infrastructure, incremental minor change through bridge strengthening, road widening and straightening with standardised, often over-engineered, solutions, the gradual suburbanisation of the countryside through streetlighting, kerbing etc, over signing, whether tourist attractions or directions signs designed to be read at speed. Such incremental change and damage is the hardest to quantify, partly because of inadequate information about the present or recent past.

The tourism industry, now the single most important industry in the Yorkshire Dales brings with it its own problems and opportunities. The mobility offered by car-ownership and a lengthening of the tourist season result in higher levels of footpath erosion, greater demands for car parking in villages and beauty spots, and increased pressure on the peaceful quality of the landscape. The Countryside and Rights of Way Act gives a right of access, on foot, to the moorlands and registered common land of the Dales but visitors must still follow the Countryside Code which is designed to minimise conflict between legitimate users of the countryside. Local restrictions may apply, particularly with regard to dogs.

Improving standards of living create a demand for more sophisticated facilities but the landscape remains the key tourist attraction. In 1989 the Landscapes For Tomorrow project asked residents and visitors about their perception of the Yorkshire Dales landscape and how it might look in the twenty-first century. Participants were asked to think about how particular features of the landscape, including walls, woodland, hay meadows and barns, and were offered seven possible scenarios of how the landscape might look depending on the application of agricultural subsidies, grants and planning policies. These scenarios ranged from a wild, naturally forested landscape set aside for wildlife, a landscape managed for sporting activities and leisure, through variations on the present landscape, to one of a mixed ranching and intensive agricultural production. The preferred landscape was one broadly similar to that of today, but with a greater density of hay-meadows and small broad leaved woodlands. Participants also expressed a willingness to pay for the creation and maintenance of such a landscape.

Conservation of the landscape, and the archaeological and cultural features within it (90), should not mean fossilisation. The Yorkshire Dales is not a museum but a working landscape that has always been in a constant state of change and, in changing, will create the historic environment of the future. The challenge for conservation is to balance often conflicting demands and to protect the special character of the landscape for present and future generations, while not forgetting that this character is a result of its exploitation and utilisation by our ancestors.

91 Grinton Lead smelt mill. Consolidation work, organised by the National Park Authority, included re-roofing the mill building and peat store and repairs to the culverted stream. The mill is popular with school parties and family groups.

GLOSSARY

ashlar Masonry of hewn or sawn stone in blocks which are carefully squared and finely jointed in level courses.

assart A small area of land, reclaimed from woodland, moorland or waste ground, and enclosed for use as arable or pasture land, normally by an individual. This process of enclosing, common at various times during the medieval period, is known as assarting.

barbed and tanged arrowhead A projectile point, made on a flint flake or blade, usually roughly triangular in shape with the base of the triangle worked with two notches to form barbs and a central tang for attaching the point to a shaft.

bercary A medieval farm specialising in sheep.

bale Also bole. An early form of wind-blown furnace for lead smelting.

chambered cairn A mound of stone, of Neolithic date, containing one or more chambers which were regularly opened to allow bodies, or parts of bodies, to be placed in the cairn.

co-axial field system A group of fields laid out on a single dominant axis, subdivided by transverse boundaries.

common pasture The right to pasture animals over common land, or over common arable fields after the crop had been harvested.

coppice A tree, or groups of trees, periodically cut back to ground level and allowed to regrow to produce successive crops of wood.

core A flint knapping term: a core is the central piece of flint from which blades and flakes are removed. Cores can be divided into various types according to the knapping technique.

cremation The practice of burning a corpse on or in a pyre (bonfire).

earthworks Banks and ditches and other irregularities in the surface of the ground caused by human construction and occupation.

enclosure Many prehistoric sites which were surrounded by a bank, wall or ditch, are commonly called enclosures by archaeologists. Enclosures vary considerably in size, from individual buildings to large enclosures for livestock. Many are subdivided and contained hut circles and other structures. In a post-medieval context 'enclosure' is used to describe the process of 'enclosing' common land which could then be farmed by a single individual or sold.

farmstead A single farmhouse with outbuildings and ancillary structures.

Flag, flagstone A heavy slab, suitable for paving or roofing, normally of sandstone.

fulling mill A mill where cloth was made heavier and more compact through beating and shrinking.

hamlet A subdivision of a township. Hamlets had specific boundaries but were not a separate area for taxation purposes.

henge A circular enclosure, with a bank outside the ditch, constructed in the Later Neolithic or Early Bronze Age, possibly for ceremonial purposes.

hillfort A fortified enclosure sited on a hilltop.

hypocaust An underfloor heating system used in Roman buildings.

inhumation The practice of placing a corpse in a grave.

leaf-shaped arrowhead A projectile point, made on a flint flake or blade, characterized by a roughly oval, leaf-shaped form, usually worked on both faces by pressure flaking or by controlled direct percussion.

leat An artificial water channel.

loomweight A circular weight, normally of clay or stone, used to provide tension for the vertical threads on a loom.

lynchet Accumulation of plough soil along a field edge, characteristically accentuated as a scarp on a slope by downward movement

mortarium A large strong bowl, generally with a spout and a flange for easy gripping, used in the Roman period for processing food. Grit was sometimes added to the inside of the bowl to strengthen it.

mullion A narrow stone or wooden column subdividing a window and providing structural support.

orthostat A large stone slab set on edge.

partible inheritance The system whereby an inheritance is divided between all heirs.

pillow mound A flat topped, rectangular, earthen mound built for farming rabbits.

pollard A tree whose branches are cut back to the trunk, above the reach of browsing animals, and allowed to regrow to produce successive crops of wood.

purlin A horizontal beam which provides intermediate support for the common rafters of a roof.

quern A stone used for grinding corn into flour by hand.

quoin A dressed stone at the external angle of a wall. Quoins are often alternately large and small.

Samian A red-coated tableware pottery imported into Britain on a vast scale during the Roman period, chiefly from Gaul (France). Also known as *terra sigillata*.

scraper A flaked stone tool with a steep blunt working edge. Many scrapers were used for processing animal hides.

shieling The huts and shelters used by herdsmen looking after their stock on summer pastures.

solar The principal private chamber in a house, often situated on an upper floor.

spindle whorl A small perforated weight, often made of animal bone, pottery, stone or lead, which weighted the hand-held spindle on which woollen thread was spun.

styca A type of copper coin minted in eighth- and ninth-century Northumbria.

transhumance The seasonal migration of pastoral people with their flocks and herds from a winter settlement to a summer pasture.

transom A horizontal member subdividing a window. cf mullion.

vaccary A medieval farm specialising in cattle.

vein An irregular intrusion of rock or minerals, differing from the surrounding rock.

villa The country residence of a Roman noble, based on a working farm and often used in conjunction with a residence in a town.

voussoirs The wedge-shaped stones used to construct an arch or vault.

wapentake An administrative unit composed of groups of townships. Wapentake courts declined in importance towards the end of the medieval period.

PLACES TO VISIT

This short section on sites and places to visit only touches on the wide range of archeological sites in the Yorkshire Dales. The best way to appreciate them is by walking: it is impossible to go for a walk in the Dales without passing through a part of the landscape modified by human endeavour with its own story to tell. Most land in the Yorkshire Dales is privately owned and forms part of a working landscape: walls and fences are there to stop sheep and cows straying; grass, heather and woodland are valuable resources for the people who earn their living from the land. The dense network of public footpaths and bridleways, however, allows the visitor close views of historic structures and walks through ancient settlements and field systems. Public rights of way, many of which are historic features in their own right, are clearly shown on the 1:25,000 scale Outdoor Leisure maps published by the Ordnance Survey. These detailed maps show field boundaries and the character of the landforms as well as many monuments and enable circular walks to be planned. Livestock and birds are easily disturbed and dogs should therefore be kept on a lead and under close control. Visitors should always seek the permission of the farmer before straying off public footpaths as the depiction of an archeological site on a map does not mean there is public access to it. Most are happy to give access when asked.

Some places illustrate the activities of our ancestors more clearly than others. A small selection of the more prominent sites which have public access, either by means of public rights of way or by special access agreements, is listed below. A charge is made for some castles and abbeys. An Ordnance Survey grid reference is given for each site, and, where appropriate, figure numbers in bold type.

Prehistoric

Victoria Cave (SD 838650) (**8, 9, 28, colour plate 1**) Nineteenth century excavations at Victoria Cave removed the archeological deposits and it is now much larger than the cave used during the Roman period. External viewing only is recommended as the rock face above the cave is frost shattered and animals and birds may dislodge pieces of rock above the entrance.

Castle Dykes Henge (SD 982873) (**11**) A Countryside Stewardship agreement provides public access to the bank and ditch of this grass covered henge, best reached by walking from the Aysgarth-Thornton Rust road at SD996882.

Maiden Castle (SE 022981) (**colour plate 5**) A public footpath runs beside part of this enigmatic hillside enclosure in Swaledale.

Ingleborough (SD 742746) (**18**) The remains of the stone rampart and the hut circles or ring cairns, as well as the views, make the climb up to Ingleborough well worthwhile. The weather at the summit is normally much more severe than in the valleys below. The shortest, but steepest walk, from just east of the Hill Inn in Chapel le Dale, passes through nature reserves.

Grassington Lea Green (SD 998655) (**colour plate 4; 27**) Half a mile north of Grassington village the Dales Way passes through a deserted medieval settlement, well-preserved co-axial field systems of prehistoric and Romano-British date and the multi-period settlement at Lea Green. The path goes past Bronze Age burial mounds and shallow shafts from early lead mining.

Gordale Scar (SD 909636) (**50**) A public footpath crosses medieval lynchets and through the centre of the earthworks of an unenclosed hut circle settlement to the west of Gordale Scar.

Roman

Malham Moor Marching Camp (SD 915655) (**22**) Mastiles Lane runs through the marching camp. A monastic cross base lies just to the north of the lane, near the centre of the camp.

Dark Age

Grinton dykes (SE 037984) (**30, 31**) The minor road west of Grinton on the south side of the Swale cuts through two dykes but they are best appreciated from the dense network of footpaths.

Sculpture

The best collections of dark age sculpture in the Yorkshire Dales can be seen in Burnsall church (SE 033615), and Wensley church (SE 092895).

Medieval

Bolton Castle (SE 033918) (**47**) The privately owned castle, where Mary Queen of Scots was imprisoned, stands immediately to the east of some of the best medieval field systems in Northern England.

Middleham Castle (SE 127876) (**36**) The stone castle at Middleham is in the care of English Heritage. A short walk along a public footpath leads to the earthworks of the privately owned motte and bailey castle, Williams Hill.

Richmond Castle (NZ 172006) (**colour plate 11**) Richmond Castle, towering above the River Swale in the centre of Richmond is in the care of English Heritage, as are the remains of the Premonstratensian Easby Abbey, about a mile downstream (NZ 184003).

Skipton Castle (SD 991520) Despite being slighted after the Civil Wars, Skipton Castle still dominates the market town which grew up around it.

Castlehaw (SD 662923) (**35**) A permissive path, starting from a roughly surfaced lane, provides access to this earthwork motte and bailey castle on the outskirts of Sedbergh.

Jervaulx Abbey (SE 172858) The ruins of this privately owned abbey are remarkable for the wide range of plants which have been encouraged to colonise them.

Bolton Priory (SE 074541) (**39**) The church is still used for worship. The Bolton Abbey estate allow access to much of the precinct of the Augustinian Priory including the tithe barn.

Barden Tower (SE 051572) (**38**) The Tower itself is now only a ruined shell but the Bolton Abbey estate allow free access to its grounds.

Norton Tower (SD 975570) A Countryside Stewardship agreement provides public access to this hunting tower and the pillow mounds of the adjacent rabbit warren. It is best reached by walking from Rylstone.

Industrial remains

Mining landscapes can be dangerous. It is always advisable to keep clear of shafts and their surrounding spoil heaps. Many abandoned shafts were only covered with wood which rots and can suddenly collapse. Levels should never be entered except in the company of experienced mining surveyors due to the dangers of roof falls and foul air. Many of the buildings associated with the lead industry are now also derelict and dangerous. The National Park Authority has carried out consolidation work on some sites although care should still be taken. Ruined walls should not be used as climbing frames.

Grinton lead smelt mill (SE 048964) (**colour plate 16, 91**) Grinton lead smelt mill originally contained three ore hearths and is remarkable for its 16m (53ft) single span roof. The peat store was built alongside the flue.

Surrender lead smelt mill (SD 991999) **(66)**
The present mill, built in 1841, originally had four hearths. Their flues merged just to the north of the mill. The ruined peat store lies to the east.

Old Gang lead smelt mill (NY 975005) **(65)**
Mining, dressing and smelting all took place at Old Gang. There are the remains of at least two smelt mills, a massive peat store, reservoirs, levels and hushes. The track up the valley, followed by the Coast to Coast path, leads to further extensive mining remains, some of which have been reworked for barytes, and into Gunnerside Gill.

Sir Francis Mine, Gunnerside Gill (SD 942996) **(62, colour plate 15)**
Large dressing floors on either side of Gunnerside Gill at Sir Francis Mine were worked by separate mining companies from the same level. Further up Gunnerside Gill are impressive hushes, dressing floors, a smelt mill and dams.

Bolton Park Mine (SE 029931) A late-nineteenth-century dressing floor, consolidated and interpreted by the National Park Authority.

Hebden – Yarnbury (SE 027646 - SE 015648) **(61, 64)** An equally impressive range of mining features including complex dressing floors, shallow and deep shafts and hushes can be seen by walking from Hebden Gill to Yarnbury. An interpretative trail links many of the mining remains on Grassington Moor.

Ribblehead (SD 765792) **(78)** The Batty Moss viaduct dominates the landscape at Ribblehead but beside the road junction can be seen the fragmentary remains of the buildings of the construction camps.

Farfield Mill (SD 677918) A nineteenth-century water-powered woollen mill complex, now run as a Heritage Centre.

Gayle Mill (SD 872894) **(75)** This purpose-built cotton mill and its unusual water supply can be easily seen from the centre of Gayle.

Craven Lime Works (SD 824663) **(72)** The remains of the Hoffmann lime kiln and two other kilns have been consolidated by the National Park Authority and can be viewed from an interpretative trail.

Toft Gate (SE 130644) An unusual commercial lime kiln with a ground level flue, recently consolidated and interpreted with a grant from the Local Heritage Initiative.

Most of these sites, and many others featured in this book, are Scheduled Ancient Monuments, protected by Act of Parliament. It is an offence to damage or to use a metal detector on a scheduled monument. Scheduling is intended to ensure that these nationally important sites survive for future generations to learn from and enjoy.

Museums and National Park Centres

The Dales Countryside Museum in Hawes, Richmond Museum, the Craven Museum at Skipton, the Grassington Folk Museum, and the Swaledale Folk Museum in Reeth all have displays relating to the archaeology and local history of the Dales. The Earby Mines Museum at Earby contains the best collection of lead mining remains.

The National Park Centres at Aysgarth, Grassington, Malham and Reeth each have different exhibitions about the Yorkshire Dales. The Dales Countryside Museum and the Centres can provide information about guided walks on archeological themes and on other sites to visit in the Yorkshire Dales, as well as information about other aspects of the Yorkshire Dales and its landscape.

Web site

A new web site, www.outofoblivion.org.uk., is based on the Historic Environment Record maintained by the Yorkshire Dales National Park Authority. Its aims are to increase enjoyment of the Dales and help the understanding of its unique cultural landscape.

FURTHER READING

The Yorkshire Dales is well served by books about its local history, geology, vegetation and topography, but not by general books about its archaeology and landscape history. Andrew Fleming's *Swaledale: Valley of the Wild River* (Edinburgh University Press, 1998) is a notable exception. *Archaeology and historic landscapes in the Yorkshire Dales*, edited by Robert White and Pete Wilson is a collection of twenty papers describing recent research, ranging from aerial survey and burnt mounds to hogg houses and reading rooms (Yorkshire Archaeological Society, 2002). Arthur Raistrick's *The Pennine Dales* (Eyre and Spottiswoode, 1968) and Richard Muir's *The Dales of Yorkshire: a Portrait* (Macmillan, 1991) provide wider ranging landscape histories. Marie Hartley and Joan Ingilby's *The Yorkshire Dales*, first published by Dent in 1956, is still one of the best general histories.

Readers interested in the geology of the area will find *Geology Explained in the Yorkshire Dales and on the Yorkshire Coast* by D. Brumhead (David and Charles, 1979), *The Face of North West Yorkshire* by A. Raistrick and J. L. Illingworth (Dalesman Publishing Co., 1967), and *Geology of the Northern Pennine Orefield, Volume 2, Stainmore to Craven* by K. C. Dunham and A. A. Wilson, (British Geological Survey, 1985) instructive. *The Vegetation of the Yorkshire Dales National Park* by A. Drewitt (Yorkshire Dales National Park Committee, 1991) is a good introduction to the vegetation and habitats of the area.

Early antiquarian investigations concentrated on the caves of the Craven area for which W. Boyd Dawkins' *Cave Hunting* (Macmillan 1874, republished by EP Publishing in 1973) provides a contemporary introduction. Arthur Raistrick, doyen of Yorkshire Dales archaeological and geological studies, drew attention to the field monuments of Craven in a series of articles in the 1920s and 1930s, mainly in the Yorkshire Archeological Journal such as 'Iron Age Settlements in West Yorkshire', (*YAJ* 34, 1939). *Archaeology in the Pennines*, edited by T. Manby and P. Turnbull, is a collection of studies in honour of Raistrick (British Archeological Reports, British Series 158, 1986).

N. Higham's *A Regional History of England: The Northern Counties to AD1000* (Longman, 1986) deals mainly with the area to the north of the Dales but provides a good regional context as does B. Hartley and L. Fitts's *The Brigantes* for the Roman period (Alan Sutton, 1988). The agricultural exploitation of the uplands is brought to life in A. Winchester's *The Harvest of the Hills: Rural Life in Northern England and the Scottish Borders, 1400-1700* (Edinburgh University Press, 2000). Prior to 1974 the Yorkshire Dales were divided between the North and the West Ridings of Yorkshire. *The Victoria County History for the North Riding* provides basic parish histories for its area. It has no direct equivalent for the West Riding although T. D. Whitaker's *The History and Antiquities of the Deanery of Craven* (3rd ed, Dodgson, 1878) is still useful. *West Yorkshire: An Archaeological Survey to AD1500*, edited by M. Faull and S. Moorhouse, covers the area to the south of the

Dales but provides very useful comparative background information (West Yorkshire Metropolitan County Council, 1981). Two books produced as a result of WEA classes provide detailed studies of smaller areas: *A History of Richmond and Swaledale*, by R. Fieldhouse and B. Jennings (Phillimore, 1978) and *A History of Nidderdale* edited by B. Jennings (Advertiser Press, Huddersfield 1983). Raistrick's *Old Yorkshire Dales*, (David and Charles, 1968) and *Arthur Raistrick's Yorkshire Dales* (Dalesman, 1991) are collections of essays about aspects of Dales history.

Detailed studies of individual aspects of the archaeology and history of the Yorkshire Dales include 'A New Survey of Ingleborough Hillfort, North Yorkshire' by M. Bowden and others (*Proceedings of the Prehistoric Society* 55, 1989), *The Romano-British Archaeology of Victoria Cave, Settle* by M. Dearne and T. C. Lord (British Archaeological Reports, British Series 273, 1998), *Bolton Priory, The Economy of a Northern Monastery, 1286-1325,* by I. Kershaw (Oxford University Press, 1973), and *Marrick Priory: A Nunnery in Late Medieval Yorkshire* by J. Tillotson (University of York Borthwick Paper 75, 1989).

More has been written on the lead industry than any other aspect of the archaeology of the area. Robert Clough's *The Lead Smelting Mills of Yorkshire Dales* (privately published in 1962), was a seminal work. M. Gill's study *Swaledale: its mines and smelt mills* (Landmark Publishing, 2001) draws on the results of more recent fieldwork and documentary research. Many volumes of British Mining, the Journal of the Northern Mines Research Society, concentrate on area studies of the industry in the Dales while the CD ROM *Cononley Mine: An Interactive Archaeological Tour* published by Martin Roe (2000) offers a new approach to making underground remains generally accessible. G. Wright's *Roads and Trackways of the Yorkshire Dales,* (Moorland Publishing Co., 1985) discusses transport but other industrial subjects are less well covered. The Hoffman Kiln at Langcliffe is described by M. Trueman in *'The Langcliffe Quarry and Limeworks'* (Industrial

Archaeology Review XIV, 2 1992). Field lime kilns are discussed in 'Limekilns in Sedbergh, Garsdale and Dent' by I. Cleasby (*Current Archaeology* 145, 1995), a summary of an award winning survey by a local group. *The lime and limestone industries of the Yorkshire Dales* by D. Johnson (Tempus, 2002) is more wide ranging.

Vernacular Houses in North Yorkshire and Cleveland by B. Harrison and B. Hutton, (John Donald, 1984) provides a detailed study of the vernacular buildings of the region, based on the work of the Yorkshire Vernacular Buildings Study Group. More recent studies are reported in the Group's annual journal, *Yorkshire Buildings*.

Folk life is well covered by the extensive work of Marie Hartley and Joan Ingilby, founders of the Dales Countryside Museum, especially their superb *Life and Traditions in the Yorkshire Dales* (Dent, 1968) while *A Dales Heritage* (Dalesman, 1982) and *Dales Memories* (Dalesman, 1986) concentrate more on social history.

Some recent work on the archaeology of the Yorkshire Dales has been published in archeological periodicals, particularly the *Yorkshire Archaeological Journal, Northern History* and *Landscape History*. *The Sedbergh Historian* has articles relating to the area of Sedbergh, Dent and Garsdale. The results of many more projects are currently only available as interim reports in CBA Forum, the annual newsletter of the Yorkshire Group of the Council for British Archaeology, or as typescript reports lodged with the Sites and Monuments Record held by the National Park. Some of the archeological conservation and management work carried out by the Authority, including a case study on Castlehaw, is described in *Erosion on Archaeological Earthworks: Its Prevention, Control and Repair*, edited by A. Berry and I. Brown (Clwydd County Council, 1994) while 'Arresting Decay: Archaeology in the Yorkshire Dales' in R. White and R. Iles (eds) *Archaeology in National Parks*, (National Parks Staff Association, 1991) concentrates more on consolidation of the remains of the lead industry.

INDEX

Grid references for places in the Dales are given in italics;
numbers in bold refer to illustrations